Israeli Settlements

Israeli Settlements

Land Politics beyond the Geneva Convention

Martin Blecher

Hamilton Books

Lanham • Boulder • New York • Toronto • London

An imprint of The Rowman & Littlefield Publishing Group, Inc.
4501 Forbes Boulevard, Suite 200, Lanham, Maryland 20706
Hamilton Books Acquisitions Department (301) 459-3366

6 Tinworth Street, London SE11 5AL

British Library Cataloguing in Publication Information Available

Library of Congress Cataloguing-in-Publication Information Available
Library of Congress Control Number: 2018957780

ISBN: 978-0-7618-7064-7 (cloth : alk. cloth)
ISBN: 978-0-7618-7065-4 (electronic)

∞™ The paper used in this publication meets the minimum requirements of American National Standard for Information Sciences Permanence of Paper for Printed Library Materials, ANSI/NISO Z39.48-1992.

Printed in the United States of America

Ephron answered Abraham, “Listen to me, my lord; the land is worth four hundred shekels of silver, but what is that between you and me? Bury your dead.”

Abraham agreed to Ephron’s terms and weighed out for him the price he had named in the hearing of the Hittites: four hundred shekels of silver, according to the weight current among the merchants.

So Ephron’s field in Machpelah near Mamre—both the field and the cave in it, and all the trees within the borders of the field—was deeded to Abraham as his property in the presence of all the Hittites who had come to the gate of the city. Afterward Abraham buried his wife Sarah in the cave in the field of Machpelah near Mamre (which is at Hebron) in the land of Canaan. So the field and the cave in it were deeded to Abraham by the Hittites as a burial site.

—Genesis 23:14-20 (NIV)

Contents

Acknowledgments

Writing this book has been a journey. I have benefited from the support, assistance, and encouragement of many people while writing this book, and it is a pleasure to have an opportunity to thank them.

I would like to pay tribute to my parents, Jan Eric and Elise Blecher. Without their lifelong guidance and wisdom I may never have understood the meaning of true commitment.

Without the help from Dr. Havatzelet Yahel from the Ben-Gurion Institute for the Study of Israel and Zionism, and Ruth Kark, Professor of Geography at Hebrew University, I would not have had the opportunity, nor the access to come across the District Court's ruling in one of the more important land cases examining the praxis of the Ottoman Land Laws, *Al-Uqbi vs the State of Israel*. The Supreme Court upheld this decision.

My friend, Eli Göndör, has tirelessly taught me that questions were the lights that illuminate the path of truth and a tool to truly see with our own eyes and not through the eyes of others.

Finally, I wish to thank my wife, Karina. She helped me, substantively and otherwise, at various stages through this journey. More importantly, she has been a steadying hand through countless other journeys along the way.

Introduction

One of the most controversial issues in international law is Israeli settlements. In relation to its question's relevance and context, there is surprisingly little comprehensive literature on the issue, without any ideological standpoint on either side. The world community has consistently determined its illegitimacy. Israeli governments, and some international professors of international law, have contested this. How should the concept of settlements be understood? What paragraphs and regulations govern each interpretation?

On the one hand, for many Israelis and Jews in the diaspora, settlements are a troubling issue to discuss. Perhaps you do not want to discuss the issue. Alternatively, one may refuse to consider the question because it is hard to answer. It is an infected question.

On the other hand, the argument goes in the opposite direction of other Israelis and Jews in the diaspora. You cannot understand the reasoning behind why, and how, holy places of the Jews can be settlements. Just as Karbala, Najaf, and Mecca are holy to Muslims; many Jews repudiate the Wailing Wall, the Temple Mount, the Mount of Olives, and Hebron as settlements. Again. An infected question; a polarizing one.

The conviction that Jewish settlements in the West Bank are illegal is now so commonly accepted, it hardly seems as though the matter is even open for discussion. But it is. Decades of argument about the issue have obscured the complex nature of the specific legal question about which a supposedly overwhelming verdict of guilty has been rendered against the Israeli settlement policy. There can be no doubt that this avalanche of negative opinion has been deeply influenced by the settlements' unpopularity around the world and even within Israel itself. From late 1960s world leaders has argued that Israeli settlements violate international law. while at the same time refused to apply the similar arguments in reference to other territorial conflicts which areas are under dispute. Yet, while one may debate the wisdom of Israeli settlements, the idea that they are imprudent is quite different from branding them as illegal.

Though routinely referred to nowadays as Palestinian land, at no point in history has Jerusalem or the West Bank been under Palestinian Arab sovereignty in any sense of the term. For several hundred years leading up to World War I, all of Israel, the Kingdom of Jordan, and the putative state of Palestine were merely provinces of the Ottoman Empire. After British-led Allied troops routed the Turks from the country in 1917–1918, the League of Nations blessed Britain's occupation with a document that gave the British conditional control granted under a mandate. It empowered Britain to facilitate the creation of a Jewish National Home while respecting the rights of the native Arab population. In 1922, British Colonial Secretary Winston Churchill partitioned the mandate and gave the East Bank of the Jordan to his country's Hashemite Arab allies, who then created the Kingdom of Jordan under British tutelage.

Following World War II, the League of Nations' successor, the United Nations, voted in November 1947 to partition the remaining portion of the land into Arab and Jewish states. While the Jews accepted partition, the Arabs did not, and after the British decamped in May 1948, Jordan joined with four other Arab countries to invade the fledgling Jewish state on the first day of its existence, May 15, 1948.Though Israel survived the onslaught, the fighting left the Jordanians in control of what would come to be known as the West Bank as well as approximately half of Jerusalem, including the Old City. The Jewish communities in the West Bank that had existed prior to the Arab invasion were demolished, as was the Jewish quarter of the Old City of Jerusalem.

After the cease-fire that ended Israel's War of Independence in 1948, Jordan annexed both the West Bank and East Jerusalem. But, as was the case when Israel annexed those same parts of the ancient city that it would win back nineteen years later, the world largely ignored this attempt to legitimize Jordan's presence. Only Jordan's allies, Britain and Pakistan, recognized its claims of sovereignty. After King Hussein's (1935–1999) disastrous decision to ally himself with Egypt's President Nasser (1918–1970) during the prelude to June 1967, Jordan was evicted from the lands it had won in 1948.

This left open the question of the sovereign authority over the West Bank. The legal vacuum in which Israel operated in the West Bank after 1967 was exacerbated by Jordan's subsequent stubborn refusal to engage in talks about the future of these territories.

International law arguments against the settlements have rested primarily upon two sources. First are the International Committee of the Red Cross (ICRC), October 18, 1907, The Hague Regulations, whose provisions are primarily designed to protect the interests of a temporarily ousted sovereign in the context of a short-term occupation. Second is the ICRCs August 12, 1949 Fourth Geneva Convention, the first international agreement designed specifically to protect civilians during wartime.[1]

While Israel was not and is not a party to The Hague Regulations, the Israeli Supreme Court has generally regarded its provisions as part of customary international law (that is, law generally observed by nations even if they have not signed an international agreement to that effect) and hence applicable to Israel. The regulations are transparently geared toward short-term occupations during which a peace treaty can be negotiated between the victorious and the defeated nations. The "Three No's" of the Khartoum Resolution, September 1, 1967—"no peace with Israel, no recognition of Israel, no negotiations with Israel"—signaled that there would be no quick negotiations.[2]

Nonetheless, Israel established and maintains a military administration overseeing the West Bank in accordance with The Hague Regulations, probably the only military power since World War II, other than the United States in Iraq, that has done so.

All of this makes it so interesting to explore. Even though The Hague Convention is of importance, the settler question is highlighted, most of all, through the same lens. Article 49 of Geneva Convention IV.

> Individual or massive transfers, as well as the deportation of protected persons from occupied territory to the Occupying Power Territory or to any other country, occupied or not, are prohibited regardless of the motive.
>
> Nevertheless, the Occupying Power can complete total or partial evacuation of a particular area if the population's security or essential military reasons so require. Such evacuations shall not mean that the protected persons are moved outside of the Occupied Territory, except for material reasons, it is not possible to avoid such displacement. Persons thus evacuated will be moved back to their homes as soon as the hostilities in the area have expired.
>
> Occupational powers that transmit or evacuate shall ensure, as far as possible, that adequate accommodation is provided to receive the protected persons, the removal takes place in satisfactory hygiene, health, safety and nutrition conditions and that members of the same family are not separated.
>
> The protective power shall be informed of any transfers and evacuations as soon as they have taken place.

> The Occupying Power must not imprison protected persons in an area that is particularly vulnerable to war's dangers unless the security of the population or essential military reasons so requires.
>
> The Occupying Power must not expel or transfer parts of its own civilian population to the territory it occupies.[3]

This article is interesting to contrast and/or complement with the other, much less-known formulations and concepts such as:

- land laws
- ownership
- the respect of the laws in force in the occupied territory.

This study aims to highlight why the Israeli settlement issue cannot and will not be simplified solely based on the above provision in the Fourth Geneva Convention, but in all fairness and straightforwardness, the issue should be understood by analyzing several different parameters, policies, and contexts. The view is not necessarily to impair the Convention's Article 49. Rather, its aim is to be understood as a complement to provide the reader with as much of a comprehensive view and knowledge of Israeli settlements as possible.

In 1968, US President Johnson's administration voiced their objection to Israeli land politics in the West Bank (Israel refers to the areas as Judea and Samaria) by invoking Article 49.[4]

Israel refutes the application of the Geneva Convention in the context of settlements on the West Bank. Since it does so, the more relevant question arise on what laws, governance, and regulations are of importance in understanding the Israelis' behavior?

On the homepage of the ICRC, the most important principles governing occupation are summed up.[5] One of the most central principles with regard to rules of Occupation is that "the Occupying Power must respect the laws in force in the occupied territory, unless they constitute a threat to its security or an obstacle to the application of the international law of occupation."[6]

And yet, this principle [as is the case with the regulation of "the Occupying Power must take measures to restore and ensure, as far as possible, public order and safety"[7]] is non-existent from the political and public discourses when a discussion of Israeli settlements is on the agenda.

Why does the political discourse place such centrality in the Geneva Convention's Article 49, while Article 43 of the Hague Convention, "The authority of the legitimate power having in fact passed into the hands of the occupant, the latter shall take all the measures in his power to restore, and ensure, as far as possible, public order and safety, while respecting, unless absolutely prevented, the laws in force in the country,"[8] that can add components of how to interpret land acquisition, is omitted in the political discourse? I want to explore how Article 43 has affected Israeli policies and positions vis-à-vis the settlements.

One ought to ask why it is of importance and value to mention Ottoman land laws, Hague Regulations and the Fourth Geneva Convention in the same context? The answer is because they correlate to one another. Equally important to the Geneva Conventions are the Hague Regulations. Regardless, if one contests the Geneva Convention´s applicability of the Israeli settlements or is supportive of its taking, it has created a legal vacuum which makes it reasonable, if not necessary, to combine Ottoman land laws, Hague Regulations and the Fourth Geneva Convention.

Since Jordan's occupation of the West Bank from 1949 through 1967 was not recognized by the international community; and Israel, as an occupier, has the duty and responsibility to respect and to uphold the laws in force in the occupied territory, it becomes relevant as to which laws it deems to uphold. Since Palestine or the Palestinian Authority, was not the prime actor prior 1967 when these areas came under Israeli control, the solution, right or wrong, came to be a combination of a set of laws.

Barbara J. Smith writes in *The Roots of Separatism in Palestine*, that the British officials charged with the mandate of Palestine, "misread the previous land laws." It is not too farfetched to assume that this misreading, in one way or another, has affected how Israeli Courts have read and interpreted land laws.[9]

It is equally true that comprehensive registration of land ownership did not exist in the West Bank in 1967; therefore, only one-third of the land had been registered.

Due to the fragmentary and incomplete system of land registration in Palestine, (which affected state land as well as other land), obstacles and further complexities arise.

Thus, I aim to survey old land laws, a heritage from the Ottoman Empire. It is my conviction that the settlement enterprise ought to be viewed from different types of lenses. By examining different source of materials, a diverse picture of how to understand a certain type of Israeli behavior will begin to evolve.

While interpretations of international law as to the legality of settlements vary according to bias, few have stopped to consider whether land could intrinsically belong collectively to an entire people. It might be that the notion of collectively owned land is what drives the peace process today and enables governments to consider racist policies of population transfer and land swaps.

Most often, the question regarding Israeli settlements is filled with dogmas and the lack of profound reasoning where one's own independent, critical thinking is a disappearing feature, blocked by repeated reasoning. That a point of view repeats itself does not always guarantee its correctness and rightfulness. Therefore, I want to include in this study as many aspects as possible about the issue of settlements without taking strong positions on which is right and which is not.

The objective is not to explore whether Israel complies with the Convention's Article 49. Rather, the purpose is to examine and understand from a view that international law is relying on several articles and laws. What has been done in regard to the Israeli settlements is that law experts almost single-handedly explore the question through one specific Article while neglected other Articles and Conventions. In doing so, the contemplator will lack a *comprehensive* understanding of why actors behave in the way they do. Even if one does not agree with Israel's policies in general, or Israel´s settlement policies in particular, I am amazed at how previous research has not sufficient explored Israel´s settlement policies through the objective of former land laws within the jurisdictive area. As noted, one can still reach the conclusion that Israel's land policies are in violation of international law even after a close reading of the Ottoman Land Laws.[10] This element is in addition to the main point of my book. I want to show that the question of Israeli settlements has been politicized through one particular understanding of the Geneva Convention, while few observers recognize and thus fail to understand that the land laws in West Bank were based on legal principles established prior to the creation of the Geneva Convention.

The purpose is to supplement already established data with less discussed material. This is a critique that former research has been too narrow in its area of exploration; I am also quite surprised that the question of land policy and laws regarding ownership of waste land and state land appear to be alien to observers interested in the Middle East.

Everything comes from somewhere. Law abiding countries don´t invent policies out of the blue. The behavior and policies derive from something and somewhere. Then there is interpretation, reinterpretation, adapting to modern needs and environment. While paragraphs from the Fourth Geneva Convention has, over decades, been thoroughly examined, few have considered other parameters over Israel's land policies.

My aspiration with writing this book is that future scholars will examine Israeli settlement policies, and land policies in general, more thoroughly through the context of different judiciaries (British, Jordanian, Israeli). Research and litterature of land laws in the Ottoman era is, with few exceptions, still quite rare.

NOTES

1. See International Committee of the Red Cross (ICRC), "Convention (IV) Respecting the Laws and Customs of War on Land and Its Annex: Regulations Concerning the Laws and Customs of War on Land. Annex to the Convention: Article 43. Section 3. Military Authority Over the Territory of the Hostile State." The Hague. October 18, 1907. https://ihl-databases.icrc.org/ihl/WebART/195-200053? (accessed May 25, 2018); and ICRC, "Convention (IV) Relative to the Protection of Civilian Persons in Time of War." Article 49. Geneva. August 12, 1949. https://ihl-databases.icrc.org/ihl/WebART/380-600056 (accessed May 25, 2018).
2. For text of the resolution, see Jewish Virtual Library, "Israel-Arab Peace Process: The Khartoum Resolutions (September 1, 1967)," https://www.jewishvirtuallibrary.org/the-khartoum-resolutions (accessed May 27, 2018).
3. ICRC, "Convention (IV)," Deportations, Transfers, Evacuations, Article 49,https://ihl-databases.icrc.org/applic/ihl/ihl.nsf/WebART/380-600056(accessed June 5, 2018).
4. Jewish Virtual Library, "Lyndon Johnson Administration: Administration Alarmed by Israeli Settlement Plans," April 8, 1968, http://www.jewishvirtuallibrary.org/administration-alarmed-by-israeli-settlement-plans-april-1968 (accessed May 25, 2018).
5. Definitions of the term "Occupation" are derived and collected from International Committee of the Red Cross (ICRC), "Occupation and International Humanitarian Law: Questions and Answers," August 8, 2004, https://www.icrc.org/eng/resources/documents/misc/634kfc.htm (accessed May 25, 2018).
6. ICRC, "Occupation and International Humanitarian Law."
7. ICRC, "Occupation and International Humanitarian Law."
8. ICRC, "Convention (IV)," Regulations Respecting The Laws and Customs of War on Land Article 43, para. 3.
9. Barbara J. Smith, *The Roots of Separatism in Palestine: British Economic Policy, 1920–1929* (Syracuse, NY: Syracuse University Press, 1993), 99.

10. For more information, see *The Ottoman Land Code*, trans. Frank Ongley (London: Forgotten Books, 2015).

Method

What are the reasons behind certain actors and behaviors? The purpose of research in general is to explore, describe, and explain how and why actors think, feel, and act. *Exploratory research* is defined as the initial research into a hypothetical or theoretical idea. This is where the researcher has an idea and wishes to research a topic seeking to understand it more deeply. An explanatory research study is an attempt to lay the groundwork that could or will lead to future studies, and also to determine what is being observed that might be explained by current existing theory. Imagine that you are blindfolded or placed in a room with complete darkness. You are not being told what is in the room but you have a suspicion that something is in there. You go on an exploring adventure in the room until you find something.

Exploratory Research can come in two major forms. Either a new topic or a new angle on a previously studied topic. A new topic is often unexpected and starling in its findings. New angles on existing topics can come from new ways of looking at things, either from a theoretical perspective or from a new way of measuring something, or both.

Since there has been little attention paid to the specific Article of 43 in the Hague Convention, "Occupying Power must respect existing laws in the occupied territory," as noted in the introduction, my intention is to bring new light to the question of Israeli settlements in an exploratory manner. The end result is not to legitimize certain behaviors or policies.

This writing, and the focus of it, is not in a position to reexamine whether or not the argument of Israeli settlements holds water when fixating it on the context and purpose of the Fourth Geneva Convention's Article 49. Rather, the point of this writing is that it be used as an informational tool that perhaps might explain why involved actors view settlements the way they do, namely the Israeli government and judicial courts. This study will also examine why these entities refuse to view Israeli settlements in the same context as the rest of the world understands them. Additionally, I hope that the reader will gain insight about the complexity of land politics. If one is able to understand what factors create problems, then we have greater possibilities to search for a solution.

Chapter One

Historical Background to Israeli Land Policy

The establishment of modern states in the Arab provinces of the former Ottoman Empire led to the elimination of one of the obstacles that had prevented state ownership of waste land during the period of Ottoman rule. Under Moslem law, the common law of the Ottoman Empire, the state did not have any legal capacity. Therefore, it could not acquire any rights or assume any obligations in private law.

The earliest international document containing a reference to the land in Palestine that was not owned by private individuals is "The Palestine Mandate," which was ratified by the Council of the League of Nations, in London on July 24, 1922. It is clear that the British authorities participating in drafting the document were aware of its content well before ratification. Article 6 of the mandate states that: "The Administration of Palestine, while ensuring that the rights and position of other sections of the population are not prejudiced, shall facilitate Jewish immigration under suitable conditions and shall encourage, in co-operation with the Jewish agency referred to in Article 4, close settlement by Jews on the land, including State lands and waste lands not required for public purposes."[1] The obvious importance of land to any settler movement was thus recognized in Article 6 of the mandate.[2]

This provided the Administration of Palestine mandate to facilitate the closing of settlements by Jews on the land. But Palestine was no America. It was an extremely small, already densely populated country with limited resources. In *The Roots of Separatism in Palestine*, Barbara J. Smith, asserts that from the outset it was obvious that the assimilation of a large Jewish agricultural community into Palestine was impossible without prejudice to the "rights and position of other sections of the population."[3] Land issues tended to revolve around the question of permanent Arab economic alienation rather than physical overcrowding. The Zionists were more politically than economically motivated in their desire to establish an agricultural community in Palestine, as was acknowledged in the Preamble to the mandate, which spoke of the "historical connection of the Jewish people with Palestine."[4] Zionist organizations played an increasingly important role in land purchasing and in the formulation of land acquisition policy for the national home of the Jewish people. The political importance of land acquisition established the fundamental principle of Zionist land policy "that all land on which Jewish colonisation takes place should eventually become the common property of the Jewish people."[5]

THE ZIONIST DIMENSION

The leaders of the Zionist movement saw in private property an invalid nation-building strategy and favored instead the land regime of public ownership. While the Zionist movement and the *Yishuv* [settlement or body of Jewish residents in the Land of Israel] held no uniform perspective on land, land in *Eretz Yisrael* [the Land of Israel] did occupy a central position in Zionist ideology and practice. The major school of thought within the Zionist movement exhibited strong non-liberal and anti-liberal tendencies reflected in their positions regarding land in Palestine. This school of thought regarded neither autonomy nor the will of the individual as the basis of their aims, but rather the interests of the collective.[6]

To understand the evolving land politics, one has to consider the longing after Zion. Zion, or Eretz Israel, is a central pillar of the Jewish religion and of Jewish group identity. As a people without a homeland for nearly 2000 years, Jews strove wherever they were to maintain a sense of vital ties to the Land of Israel. They prayed for rain in Eretz Israel during the rain-abundant seasons in the countries in which they resided; they celebrated the annual harvest festival according to the seasonal agricultural cycle in Eretz Israel; and they studied the body of law governing agriculture that applies to Eretz Israel.

The ideal of settling the land had its roots in European thinking who romanticized both nature and peasantry, the beautification of the workingman. Aliyah,[7] which is the traditional Hebrew word for Jewish immigration to the Land of Israel connotes the return home of exiles, refugees adrift for generations. As a concept, like other ideals, Zionism was forced to transform. This was both in response to modern industrialism, but another explanation has to do with the intense persecution of Jews. Zionism went from being a hope into a pressing obligation. A Jew should not solemn return to its homeland, but to the land itself, to the earth.

The Jewish National Fund (JNF) was the executive organ of the Zionist movement for Jewish land purchases in Palestine, and it pursued its activities under the principle of the Jewish people's common ownership of the land.[8] The JNF was established in 1901 at the Fifth Zionist Congress through a proposal made by Zvi Hermann Shapira in Heidelberg. The idea was to create a fund for the purpose of acquiring Jewish territory. The money for acquiring the territory would come from world Jewry, and the fund would be characterized by two central pillars: (1) it was to be perpetual, and (2) the land acquired had to be forever the common and inalienable property of the Jewish people. It should not be sold to individuals but rather leased for renewable periods of no more than forty-nine years to those who were willing to work for it.

Parties and political groups affiliated with the Workers' Movement[9] were suspicious of private ownership as the means of production, and especially of the private ownership of land. Furthermore, religious elements that cited biblical and other religious sources that sanctified the Holy Land had an impact not only on religious Zionists, but also on the Zionist movement as a whole. The two pillars manifested links between modern Zionism and traditional Jewish values. The principle of land inalienability equalized the biblical notion of the Land of Israel as divine property and that according to Leviticus 25:23, it "must not be sold permanently, because the land is mine."[10] The JNF took this verse as its motto.[11] The other aspect of the principle of land inalienability was the forty-nine-year lease, which corresponded to the biblical jubilee law, according to which all lands are redeemed every fiftieth year and restored to their original owners at no cost.[12]

The policy of public land ownership was intended to prevent, or at least control, speculators by keeping the responsibility for all Jewish land in Palestine in the hands of the JNF. By putting as much land as possible under national ownership, the land would cease being a marketable commodity to be bought and sold at will. In addition, the JNF as a major buyer had the advantage of being able to buy large tracts of land that were mostly uncultivated and therefore relatively inexpensive, and in addition, it would be in a favorable position to influence land prices.

Private ownership was frowned upon for reasons of social ideology. Zionist ideology drew its inspiration both from egalitarian doctrines heralded from European socialism and from the ancient call of the prophets of Israel. Theodor Herzl, the father of political Zionism, depicted the new Jewish society as founded for the most part on cooperatives, with the most modern labor legislation. Herzl and other Zionist thinkers sought to connect classic economic theory with socialist thought. "Public land ownership and the holding of large tracks of lands by the JNF were seen as an antidote to the formation of large private estates, and consequently, the introduction of the social ills of the exploitation of human labor and the creation of a land-starved agricultural workforce."[13]

Another reason for advocating collective land ownership originated with the goal of transforming as many Jews as possible into farmers. The emphasis of Zionism upon agricultural settlements derived from two objectives. One was the important role of agriculture as a means by which to increase the area under Jewish ownership. The Zionist movement sought a cheap and fast way to expand Jewish presence. Agriculture was considered the most efficient way of establishing an extended Jewish territorial basis in Palestine, since it required less investment in physical and human capital and a shorter turnaround period than did endeavors such as manufacturing. The second was that agricultural settlements also provided an economic framework by which to absorb a large influx of Jewish immigrants who were expected to arrive in Palestine.

Kedar emphasizes that three fundamental assumptions characterized Zionist ideology near the end of the Palestine Mandate: (1) "land belongs to the collective and not to individuals; (2) this collective has a special connection to the Jewish people as a whole; and (3) this collective does not include all inhabitants of Palestine, but rather the Jews alone.[14]"

An interesting angle of private ownership is offered by journalist Orit Arfa in her article noting: "Currently, in Israel 'proper' (within the Green Line), only 7 percent of the land is owned privately by individuals (3 percent Jews and 4 percent Arabs). According to the Israeli NGO Regavim, the rest is owned by the Jewish state (80 percent) and the Jewish National Fund (13 percent). Israeli citizens lease the land in 49-98 year instalments from the Israel Land Authority. Should the government repeal the lease, they are subject to eviction."[15]

Arfa informs that "approximately 30 percent of land in WB/JS [West Bank/Judea Samaria] is classified as Israeli state land, while the rest is unsurveyed (without proven ownership) or privately owned. Of the privately-owned land, approximately 95 percent belongs to Arabs and 5 percent to Jews."[16] Since the

> Supreme Court of Israel has adopted Ottoman-turned-British Mandate law which assumes that cultivated land in WB/JS belongs to someone . . . enables Arab individuals, families, and tribes to settle and acquire unsurveyed land through consistent cultivation. For example, Arab-planted olive tree orchards dominating the landscape have been rendered 'Arab' land, which, contrary to misconceptions, Israel does not uproot. Jews, on the other hand, do not have the same rights, and Jewish agriculture on unsurveyed land does not grant Jews private ownership of it.[17]

Arfa speculates whether "one reason why Israel does not transfer or sell public land to individuals is to ensure the collective Jewish claim to the land (which it could easily rescind). Jews the world over could feel they have a stake in the land, without purchasing or cultivating it." Arfa's senses the ambiguity herself by remarking that "many of these Jews prefer to live in countries that respect the idea of private land ownership, a characteristic of modern, free countries."[18]

If both Israel and Palestinians would adopt policies of private land ownership, Arfa speculates that the likelihood of peace increases than it would

> if we were to uproot anyone from their homes. First, it would break both sides out of the harmful, irrational and hopeless "Jewish versus Arab land" continuum. Jews and Arabs who value the land would either have to purchase it or cultivate it, and in essence assume productive, rational care of it. Their moti-

vation—religious, nationalistic, or financial—matters less than if their intentions are peaceful. Criminals, terrorists, and aggressors, particularly those who use their property to kill and maim, potentially forfeit the state's protection of their property.

Of course, the concept of private land ownership raises many new questions but also many new solutions.

With individuals owning land, disputes would be taken out of the nationalistic sphere and off the international stage. They'd be settled privately—not between nations—in lower, local courts, as in the rest of the world. With the Israeli Supreme Court adjudicating land disputes, the entire nation of Israel is potentially implicated in any verdict, which is one reason why Jewish settlement in WB/JS tears apart the Jewish community, with Jews quick to distance themselves from "settlers." Naturally, both Arab and Jewish leadership would have to respect private property for this paradigm shift. Perhaps this principle should be the touchstone in any conflict resolution. Would either governing body respect the property of its individual citizens or lawful residents?

In such a scenario, individuals would be freer to live their own lives, without constant fear of arbitrary demolition, with all peoples making the best of their resources and working together to keep what they worked so hard to own. [19]

FROM MARKET TRANSACTIONS TO STATE EXPROPRIATION

As Holzman-Gazit notes, "Until independence, the Zionist movement could acquire land in Palestine only through market transactions. Political independence and sovereignty over a national territory led to a dramatic change in the Zionist strategy for land acquisition."[20]

In the 1948 war Israel obtained military "control over 77 percent of the land"[21] of the Palestine Mandate. However, this military and political victory did not for the most part imply legal ownership of—as opposed to sovereignty over- the land. "By the end of the war, Jewish individuals and organizations," among them JNF, "owned approximately 8.5 percent of the total area of the State of Israel. With the addition of state owned land, land under Jewish ownership accounted for only about 13.5 percent of Israeli territory. In other words, the State of Israel was faced from its inception with the serious problem that the overwhelming majority of national territory was legally owned by persons who could reasonably be regarded as hostile to the State and to the interests of the majority of its citizens."[22]

> Israel maintains a system of land tenure which is unusual for a country with an advanced economy. Approximately 93 percent of Israel's total land area is owned by the state and by public bodies, and by law cannot be sold to individuals. Although the institution of public land ownership is recognized in the Western world, no other democratic country runs a land regime which freezes the vast majority of the land area under ownership of the state and national institutions.
>
> The roots of Israel's tenure system date back to the period of Ottoman rule. The Ottomans, who governed the country from 1516 until the end of World War I, established a feudal tenure system in Palestine, based on the institution of state-owned land. The Ottoman institution of state ownership of land is rooted in Islamic religious law. The Koranic decree that "To God belongs all that is in heaven and in the earth" has been understood in Islamic law to mean that individuals can be neither the absolute owners nor the unfettered possessors of land and its resources.[23]

In *New Perspectives on Property and Land in the Middle East*, editor Roger Owen states that "The [Ottoman] Land Code of 1858 which was the central piece of legislation on landed property in the nineteenth century . . . , was highly revealing of the politics of property in the mid-nineteenth century Ottoman Empire."[24] The text of the Land Code around "individual ownership rights were highly fluid, continually contested and subject to qualifications."[25] "The central government was concerned with maintaining continuity in cultivation and therefore a continuous flow of taxes."[26] Owen goes on: "The Code restricted the absolute rights of owners through the provision that the land reverted to the state in the event of the owners' failure to cultivate it for three years." Furthermore, "the Code did not discourage confiscation, through the stipulation that the appropriator pay the *tapu* (title) fees and cultivate the land." It is quite likely that this "was a measure to tie the title holder to the land, to motivate him to retain possession of it" as the " the way the central government perceived individual ownership as closely related to the creation of wealth and therefore of taxable income."[27]

THE ISRAELI SUPREME COURT

The law courts constitute a separate, independent unit within the Israeli Ministry of Justice. The organization of the Courts of Law in Israel include:

- The Supreme Court
- The District Courts of Law
- The Magistrates Courts (the first instance), and in general, the Court of Traffic Offenses, Family Courts, and Juvenile Courts
- National Labor Court
- Regional Labor Courts

The Israel Ministry of Foreign Affairs describes the judiciary and court system as follows:

> The judiciary acts as Israel's watchdog over the rule of law and individual rights, as do similar institutions in other countries. However, the absence of a complete written constitution, including a bill of rights, combined with regulations remaining from British Mandatory rule and the wide powers of the legislative branch, places the judiciary in Israel in a more important and delicate position.

> The judicial system in Israel is divided into two main types: one, the general law courts which are known as civil or regular courts, and the other, tribunals and other authorities with judicial powers. The difference between the two types of institutions is, inter alia, in the extent of their jurisdiction: while jurisdiction of the law courts is general, the jurisdiction of the other tribunals is limited in terms of persons or matters or in both aspects.

Israel is a unitary state with a single system of general law courts.

> The Basic Law: The Judiciary establishes three levels of courts: the Supreme Court, district courts and magistrates' courts. The latter two are trial courts, while the Supreme Court is essentially an appellate court, which also operates as the High Court of Justice. There are no juries in Israel.[28]

According to the description by Eyal Benvenisti, in the new 2004 edition of *The International Law of Occupation*, "the Israeli Supreme Court in its capacity as the High Court of Justice adjudicates complaints against the Israeli public administration." In successive decisions, "the Court made it clear that its jurisdiction over occupation measures was mandated by law, and independent of government consent."[29] It has declared its competence, under Israeli law, to assess the measures of the military administration in the territories in light of The Hague Regulations, as customary international law. However, the Court does not view itself as empowered to examine the administration's conduct under the Fourth Geneva Convention. This is not due to doubt as to whether or not the convention applies to the West Bank and Gaza. Rather it has to do with the fact that that the Court views the convention as constitutive treaty law, and under Israeli law, only customary international law is automatically incorporated into Israeli law.

The jurisdiction exercised by the Israeli Supreme Court is unique. Although the legality of occupation measures has been examined by courts on various occasions, in no prior occupations were such measures scrutinized by a home court of the occupant that was competent to prevent them from taking effect. The government's readiness to have its measures adjudicated was explained as being motivated both by humanitarian concerns and by the wish to intensify ties between the local residents and the Israeli system, encouraging them to have faith in the Israeli legal system. The Court was also concerned with humanitarian considerations when it decided to allow petitions of inhabitants of the territories.

In extending its jurisdiction to the territories, the Supreme Court stated that it would pursue humanitarian concerns, even giving them precedence over traditional international norms that called for conservation of *status que ante*.[30]

This ideal vision did not persist. Unbridgeable conflicts between Arab and Israeli interests, particular in matters of security and Jewish settlement in the Territories, put the Court in a difficult position, and it was not always conceived as giving equal weight to interests of occupied community.

One important trait in the Supreme Court's jurisprudence was its stated policy of deference to the discretion of the military authorities whenever the latter invoked security considerations. When those cases appeared, the scrutiny was usually confined to an examination of whether the reasons cited were true or dominant motives or steamed from illegal or irrelevant considerations. The policy in question was not unique to matters concerning the occupied territories. It was consistent with the Court's decisions regarding internal Israeli matters that involved claims to security considerations cited by the authorities within Israel.

Because of the continuing state of war in the region, terrorist activities, and frequent clashes between soldiers and demonstrators, security reasons were much more frequently invoked with respect to measures taken in the territories.

When security reasons were not invoked the Court was able to apply the general criteria of Israeli administrative law, such as the relevance of considerations, impartial, nondiscrimination and reasonableness.

> The settlement of Jews in the territories was perhaps the single most controversial issue within the Israeli body politic in connection with the administration of the territories .. . petitions against the expropriation of lands (for the sole purpose of erecting settlements) put the Court in a politically difficult position . . . the Court openly acknowledged its concerns with the adverse political implications of its rulings. In the only case where a settlement project was declared illegal, the *Elon Moreh* case, Justice Landau, D.P., observed:
>
> It is. . . . Greatly to be feared that the Court will appear to be abandoning its proper place and descending into the arena of public debate, and that its decision will be received by one part of the public with acclamation and by another part with utter emotional rejection. In this sense, I regard myself here as bound by the obligation to decide in accordance with the law in every matter duly brought before the Court, knowing well from the outset that the public at large will not pay attention to the legal reasoning but only to the final conclusion, and the proper status of the Court as an institution, beyond the disputes which divides the public, is likely to be prejudiced. But what can we do, this is our task and duty as judges.[31]

DIFFERENT LAWS

Under Israeli law, the power to expropriate land is conferred upon the state and upon local authorities through two principal statues: the Land Ordinance of 1943 (Acquisition for Public Purposes) and the Planning and Building Law of 1965.[32] Needless to say, the Land Ordinance was an authoritarian and undemocratic piece of legislation. It was typical of its era and of its colonial settings. It has never been amended by the Israeli legislature and basically it still stands as it did in 1943.

The Ottoman category of state-owned land remained intact during the period of British rule in Palestine. The British, who governed the country under military rule from 1918 to 1922, did not seek to make radical changes in the local legal system. After the establishment of the Palestine Mandate of 1922, the British continued to maintain the status quo, out of concern for the potential consequences of reform to the religious foundations of Ottoman law. The British government issued "Palestine: The Palestine Order in Council," in August 1922, which proclaimed that the Ottoman law which existed in Palestine on November 1914, should remain in force, unless practical difficulties arose.[33]

During the first few years of their rule, the British attempted to stabilize the Ottoman system of land registration. However, these efforts were unsuccessful. In the same period, Zionist organizations exerted pressure on the British government to implement a comprehensive land survey in order "to help locate fallow, abandoned State land on which Jews would be able to establish settlements in the spirit of the Balfour Declaration."[34] They also supported the implementation of a process for settling a land title that would strengthen the reliability of property rights to help facilitate the purchase of privately held land. The combination of Jewish possession and undisputed ownership of land in the expanding areas of Palestine was conceived as an important means of Zionist realization of Jewish sovereignty in Palestine.

On Israel's independence in 1948, the Ottoman land categories were absorbed into Israeli law.

"Some forty new laws were adopted in the first two decades, in order to transfer ownership of conquered Palestinian Arab lands to the state of Israel and make it available for the benefit of its Jewish majority."[35]

In the District Court's ruling in Beersheba, in of the more important cases in terms of land acquisition, it is written

> The Acquisition Law is a statute that must be viewed against the background of the period in which it was enacted during the early years of the State. There is no doubt that it is a Law with special characteristics and distinct from other expropriation laws. The Law involves and is interlaced with all the essence of those early days of the State in which land was seized without a statutory basis for doing so, and the Minister of Finance was entitled retroactively under the Law to determine that the Land was required for "purposes of essential development, settlement or security" even in the absence of a statutory basis for this.[36]

The Law granted retroactive validity to the seizure of lands by the State Authorities in the period between the establishment of the State and April 1, 1952. Section 2(a) of the Acquisition Law provides that a property consisting of expropriated land shall be bestowed to the Development Authority by virtue of a certificate signed by the Minister in which the Minister testifies to three conditions having been satisfied in relation to the property:

- That on April 1, 1952 the property was not in the possession of its owners;
- the property was used or assigned for the purposes of essential development, settlement or security within the period between May 14, 1948 and April 1, 1952;
- the property is still required for one of these purposes.[37]

It is further stated, in the District Court's ruling that the

> arrangement prescribed in the Acquisition Law for the expropriation of the land in favour of the Development Authority is intended to achieve a dual purpose: on the one hand, it is designed to grant retroactive legal validity to the seizure of land by the State for the purposes of development, settlement and security in relation to land abandoned by its owners in the period following the establishment of the State, and on the other hand it is designed to provide a compensation mechanism for the landowners whose lands were expropriated. . . . The harsh nature of

> the provisions of the Acquisition Law and the non-use of the expropriation of land arrangements prescribed in the Land Ordinance, can only be understood from the aspect of the special historical circumstances of the early days of the State; against the background of the needs of the time and when lands were abandoned by their owners as a result of the events of the war.[38]

"The decision as to whether ownership rights exist over land is taken on the basis of substantive law. This law obliges the ownership claimant to prove an allocation from the authorities—whether the Ottoman authorities, the British Mandate, or the State of Israel. When founded, the State of Israel did not change previous laws regarding land ownerships."[39]

Thus, it continued to implement the existing laws: the substantive land law and the procedure land law. While the first is basically an Ottoman law with British adaptation and additions, the latter is mainly a British creation—The Land (Settlement of Title) Ordinance 1928. With a few changes, the Land (Settlement of Title) Ordinance (1928) has constituted the basis of Israel's legal system with regard to land through the present day.[40]

The Land Title settlement aims to investigate the transfer of rights according to specific procedures until it reaches back to the original source. The outcome of the process is "Title Registration," which is decisive, conclusive, and open to the public.

In summary: what shaped the realities of Israel's land policy were both the Land Ordinance inherited from the British, and the Ottomans and its Acquisition Law.

"In the early 1920s and, to a large extent, to the present, in Judea and Samaria (West Bank), state ownership had several legally significant attributes. The person in possession (*tasarruf*) of state land had no right to let the land lie fallow or to turn the land into a graveyard. Additionally, the person in possession could neither dedicate the land as an endowment (*waqf*), nor bestow it by will."[41] Special succession laws govern *miri* land.

THE DIFFERENCE IN LEGAL STATUS OVER THE LAND

According to Smith,

> Many of the disputes over Zionist land purchases concerned the legal status of the land. . . . arguments over land law were normally the effect rather than the cause of the basic problem facing the Palestine Administration: if the land was occupied and the occupiers depended on it for a livelihood, as was the case with most private and so-called state land, how were the Jewish immigrants to be accommodated without interfering with the rights of the existing population?
>
> The British Palestine Administration inherited Ottoman land law . . . which had been adapted during the nineteenth century in response to changing economic and political conditions. When the British took over, the state still retained considerable control over the disposition of most categories of agricultural land. . . . Under Ottoman law, there were five main categories of land: *mulk, miri, waqf, mewat* and *metrukeh.*[42]

Mulk

Private, or freehold land, was located mostly in urban areas, while the majority of agricultural land was classed as *miri*, over which a heritable right of position or sale was granted by the state to a private person, although the ownership remained with the state.

Miri

Miri land was out of effective control of the state as long as the tax was paid and there was a further provision that the land should not remain fallow for three consecutive years without a legal reason met.

In the case of *Al-Uqbi v. The State of Israel*, it is explained that for land to be considered Miri land pursuant to the Ottoman Land Code, it must be demonstrated that at some point it was assigned to some person by the authorities.[43]

Prior to the legislation of the Ottoman Land Code, the rights of land possession and use in and to Miri land were granted by tenants appointed by the Ottoman administration. The tenants were responsible for collecting taxes in consideration for the use of the land. At some stage, the Ottoman authorities reached the conclusion that those tenants were misusing their position and exploiting the farmers who were cultivating the lands for which they were responsible. Therefore, the tenant regime was cancelled and in its stead another regime was instated, pursuant to which the right to use Miri land was granted directly by the State and the taxes in consideration for the use of the land were paid directly to its purse, without the tenants' brokerage.

Section 3 of the Ottoman Land Code describes *Miri* land as:

> State land, the legal ownership of which is vested in the Treasury, comprises arable fields, meadows, summer and winter pasturing grounds, woodland and the like, the enjoyment of which is granted by government. Possession of such land was formerly acquired of sale or being left vacant, by permission of or grant by feudatories (sipahis) of "timars" and "ziamets" as lords of the soil, and later through the "multezims" and "muhassils". This system was abolished and possession of this kind of immovable property will henceforward be acquired by leave of and grant by the agent of the Government appointed for the purpose. Those who acquire possession will receive a -deed bearing the Imperial Cypher. The sum paid in advance (muajele) for the right of possession which is paid to the proper Official for the account of the State, is call the Tapu fee.[44]

Thus section 3 of the Ottoman Land Code tells us that in order to prove that at hand is *Miri*-classified land, it is necessary to demonstrate that it was, at some point in time, assigned by the authorities to the use of a private individual.

However, due to the many flaws of the Ottoman registration method, there were in fact Miri lands that were also possessed by private individuals without a *Kushan* [title deed] and without having been registered as such in the old land registers

The ruling in the Al Uqbi Tribe further states that even the pure assumption that Lots is *Miri* defined land, it is inadequate as burden of proof. The Supreme Court ruling tells us that the necessity of proving the terms and conditions in order to create a claim by virtue of a period of prescription, neither under Section 20 nor even under Section 78 of the Ottoman law, was not meet.

In order to acquire rights under Section 20 or under Section 78 of the Ottoman Land Code (together with Section 22 of the Prescription Law), continuous possession of land for a period of at least fifteen years, or twenty years if it began after March 1, 1943, is required. It is additionally vital under Section 78 that the possession of the land shall be accompanied by significant cultivation thereof by the possessor.

Article 78 of the Land Code:

> If a person has possessed miri or Mevkufé (land possessed in mortmain but tenanted by a kind of copyhold) for ten consecutive years without disturbance, his prescriptive right becomes proved, and whether he has a title deed (kushan) or not—such land cannot be looked upon as Mahlul (abandoned) but a new Tapu Sened (title deed) should be given to him gratis. But if he admits that such land was Mahlul and he took it without right, no consideration will be paid to the passage of time, but the land will be offered to him for its Tapu [gross] value, and if he refuses it will be sold by auction to the candidate.[45]

Article 78 of the Ottoman Land Code facilitated quick and simple acquisition of property rights for public land with the fulfillment of three cumulative conditions[46] : (1) the elapse of a period of ten years, (2) possession, and (3) cultivation. This legal recognition alarmed the authorities. Much of the motivation for speeding up the settlement process was the fear that Arab landowners would acquire rights in the land on the basis of Article 78 of the Ottoman

Land Code. One way to curtail this possibility was the enactment of the law of the Limitation in 1958.[47]

As explained by Article 78 of the Ottoman Land Code, the state has a clear economic interest in allocating *Miri* land for private use and that this land be constantly cultivated, since cessation of cultivation would mean that there is no tithe to be collected.

Most of the land that Israel has declared government property is *Miri*, rather than *Mewat*. "By the time of the British Mandate period, most West Bank land was already considered *Miri*. This is due to the fact that the land located more than 2.5 km from a village is not necessarily *Mewat*, since there might be another village on the other side that is closer."[48]

> Under Jordanian rule, cultivators had enjoyed extensive rights of possession and use of *Miri* lands. These lands were distinguished from other State lands. Under Israeli occupation, the burden of proof for the registration of Miri lands was made more stringent. This applied particularly to providing proof of cultivation for a period of 15 years (the "prescription" period). Similarly, if Palestinians could not prove that they had cultivated their Miri lands for three consecutive years, these lands were redefined as abandoned and confiscated as State lands.[49]

Waqf

Waqf was a means of dedicating land or property and its income to a religious or charitable organization or to a particular family.

Mewat

Mewat land was also under state control and is referred to as uncultivated land, including woodland and grazing lands, situated at least 1.5 miles from any settlements, for which no title deeds were issued. "In Article 6 of the British Mandate, waste land is treated as having a status equal to that of state lands. In the same way as the term state land indicates ownership by the state, 'waste land' logically refers, not only to the use of the land, but also to its ownership."[50]

Article 103 of the Ottoman Land Law:

> The expression dead land (*mewat*) means vacant (*khalt*) land, such as mountains, rocky places, stony fields, pernallik and grazing ground which is not in the possession of anyone by title-deed nor assigned ab antiquo to the use of the inhabitants of a town or village, and lies at such a distance from towns and villages for which a human voice cannot be heard at the nearest inhabited place. Anyone who is in need of such land can, with the leave of the Official, plough it up gratuitously and cultivate it on condition that the legal ownership (raqabe) shall belong to the Treasury. The provisions of the law relating to other cultivated land shall be applicable to this kind of land also. Provided that if anyone, after getting leave to cultivate such land, and having had it granted to him, leaves it as it is for three consecutive years without valid excuse, it shall be given to another. But if anyone has broken up and cultivated land of this kind without leave, there shall be exacted from him payment of the tapou value of the piece of land which he has cultivated and it shall be granted to him by the issue of a title-deed.[51]

This view is an interesting to contrast with Ya'akov Meron's.[52] As a former senior advisor on the Law of Arab Countries, and a representative of Ministry of Justice in Israel, Meron wrote an essay, "Waste Land (Mewat) in Judea and Samaria," on the land conditions in Judea and Samaria (West Bank).

In this 1981 essay on Mêwat, Meron makes it clear that no expropriation is needed for the establishment of Israeli settlements on land, referred to as waste land (Mêwat). This kind of land simply has no proprietor. The competent authority, at present the Military Governor, must merely be satisfied that the settlers will vivify the waste land. This is the sole requirement for the issuance of a government permit, which must be obtained prior to the vivification of waste land both under Article 103 of the 1858 Ottoman

Land Law, and under Section 15 of the 1965 Jordanian Management of State Property Law.

Meron based his argument (on the latter law) that under previous State Property Laws there is reference neither to lands held merely in "possession" nor to land "not surveyed nor fixed on maps of the Lands and Survey Department." It is only through the vivification of the waste land that the state may obtain ownership rights. Prior to vivification, under the 1921 Mewat Land Ordinance and the 1961 Preservation of State Lands and Properties Law, the state has no more than bare control. After vivification, and consequent state ownership, the vivifier could only lease the land. Meron thus concludes that both under 1965 Jordanian Management of State Property Law and under Ottoman Land Law it is confirmed that waste land is not owned by any state in the West Bank.

"The Jordanian Government that formerly occupied Judea and Samaria never appropriated the waste lands in those territories. . . . Similarly, the courts under the British Mandate were not particular in applying the restriction of the 1921 *Mewat* Land Ordinance. Under this restriction, only vivification completed before this Ordinance was acquisitive for individuals."[53]

However, a consequence of abandoned ownership for three successive years, is that *Mewat* (uncultivated land) became *Miri land* [land with a heritable right of position or sale was granted by the state to a private person, although the ownership remained with the state][54] .

Mewat is land that meets all the following four conditions:

1. it is wasteland
2. it is not registered in anybody's name
3. it was not assigned to residents of a specific locality or village; and
4. when standing in *Mewat* land, the loudest yell of a person cannot be heard in any inhabited place. Land that does not

> meet even one of these conditions cannot be considered to be *Mewat*.[55]

Israel's Supreme Court ruled that in light of the ambiguity in the definition of the term *Mewat* in the Ottoman Land Code, the physical-distance criterion (mile and a half) should be used alone, and not the imprecise "loudest yelling distance," which as previously noted, varies depending on topography and other physical characteristics of the land. BADIL and COHRE accuses Israel of redefining what constituted *Mewat* lands to prevent their conversion to *Miri* lands.[56]

"The extent of waste land in Judea and Samaria [West Bank] is very large. In 1935, it was observed that '[a] very large part of the area of Palestine is *Mewat*.'"[57] B'Tselem however contest this.[58]

In the District Court's ruling between the plaintiff Suleiman Mahmud Salaam El-Uqb and the Israeli state as the defendant the question whether it is deemed possible to acquire rights in *Mewat land* arises. The ruling states the following: The Land (Mewat) Ordinance of 1921 changed the Ottoman Land Code, and emphasized the need to obtain a permit from the authorities as well as the anticipated criminal sanction upon a breach of such obligation: "A person who fences off or cultivates desolate land without the consent of the lands administration department, will not be entitled to obtain a Kushan deed as to such land, and furthermore such a person can expect to be prosecuted for trespass. Any person that cultivates such land in the future without a license must notify the Land Registration Records Officer within two months and apply for a registration certificate."[59] The Land Ordinance provided a final opportunity for the registration of Mewat land, which had been revived, by giving notice within two months of publication of the Ordinance. Rights of title are not acquired in a general way and the authorities decided to put matters in order by granting a period of grace to whoever had revived and cultivated dead land, but the condition for this was, as stated, the giving of notice to the Land Registrar.

The act of appropriation could take the form of vivification of the waste land. This was the only mode of acquisition of waste land under the Ottoman Land Law. Modern States with legal capacity could also appropriate available waste land, not only through vivification, but also by registration in the Land Registry in the name of the State and by legislative action. Without an act of appropriation, waste land could not become state land. This is consistent with the rule that an individual with legal capacity could not claim ownership of waste land before appropriating it through vivification.

That the fact that waste land is distinct from state lands is confirmed by the examination of the 1858 Ottoman Land Law and the Ottoman Civil Code both of which remained in effect through June 6, 1967, when Israeli forces entered the West Bank.[60]

The British assumed total control of *Mewat* land in the mandate of Palestine but these were for the most part uncultivable. Out of British control, although still considered state property, was *Matruka* lands, held in common for use either of the public (such as roads, rivers) or for a village or a group of communities for grazing or woodcutting.

The Palestine Administration directly controlled only a small proportion of the agricultural land in Palestine. Pressure of Zionist land acquisition led it to intervene to exert certain legal controls over transfers of all types of agricultural land. The Administration's rapid introduction of new legislation governing land transfers was prompted by the political necessity for concrete action in fulfilling the pledge to help secure the establishment of the Jewish National Home.

The announcement of the Land Transfer Ordinance in September 1920 reversed a 1918 ordinance prohibiting all transfers of immovable property. The principal reason given for the closure of the land registries in 1918, aside from the fact that many registers were missing or destroyed, was the financial chaos and severe indebtedness of the peasantry caused by the war. By 1920, the economic situation was no less serious, but it was felt that the prohibition of land transfers was preventing economic growth and discouraging much needed capital investment.

FAILURE TO PROTECT ARAB PEASANTRY AND THE ENTERING OF ZIONIST SETTLERS

The Civil Administration, under its first high commissioner Sir Herbert Samuel (1920-1925), had the vision of British administrators and Jewish settlers working together for the positive development of the region. "Although Samuel's vision of the future development of Palestine obviously sought to promote the Jewish National Home policy and included provision for continued expansion of the Zionist element in the population, it was always propagated on the basis of its promise of multiethnic prosperity and benefit for all Palestinian inhabitants." Samuel's "persistently argued the political expediency of accelerating the development of the country and of crediting the Jews openly for their active role in this progress."[61] Early on in his term he emphasized that the development works contemplated would benefit the Jew and Arab alike and would tend to obviate any chance of trouble. However, as noted by Martin Bunton, "as the consequences of a market in land became clearer to the Palestinian government, particularly in the wake of the 1929 riots, there was increasing tension between the general desire to facilitate transactions in land and the fear that individualization of rights was in fact leading to social dislocation and the growth of a landless class."[62]

The departure from the Ottoman Law principle which allowed a corporation to own immovable property under certain conditions was an advantage to the Zionist land-purchasing organizations which had undoubtedly been established for the purpose of developing and establishing closer settlements of the land in Palestine.

Smith's book attest that British legislation failed to protect the Arab peasantry while it simultaneously opened the door to Jewish purchase of private land and created the opportunity for Zionist settlers to establish a land base.

No single pledge in the Mandate weighed more heavily on the British Administration than the Clause 6 of the mandate that promised to facilitate Jewish settlement on "state lands and land not required for public purposes."[63] The significance of these lands in the creation of the Jewish National Home had more to do with political prestige than with the actual fact of land acquisition, and this ensured that any transactions in such land would become the subject of exaggerated public interest on both the Zionist and the Arab sides. It is worth pointing out that state lands represented only a small proportion of Jewish land acquisition. These lands, however, had the added attraction, like those of the large absentee landholders, of being situated in the more fertile plains and valleys. The British Administration was adamant about not losing control of these state lands and, perhaps more importantly, interested in the increased income that would accrue as land prices and rents rose. Whereas under Ottoman rule it had been possible to purchase tracts of state lands under *Miri* lands, and lands of which the Zionists had entered into negotiations with pre-war authorities; therefore, the High Commissioner Sir Herbert Samuels convinced London of the advisability of immediately granting long-term leases.

The "British officials misread the previous land laws" and also "failed fully to understand local agricultural practices . . . they were under the impression that large quantities of land were vanishing from their control. Officials neglected to account for the practice of allowing land to lie fallow two years out of three, which meant that their calculations as to how much and what land was uncultivated differed widely from those of the actual cultivators."[64] The British administrators, due to their failure to acknowledge that large amount of lands had been reclaimed but not registered (registration would have required the cultivator to pay an initial fee and tax to produce the land which was often a great burden), wrongly concluded that this was the result of recent encroachment. Much of the land had been left fallow during the war because of the impoverishment of the Arab peasantry, and the so called "encroachment" was often no more than the reclamation of previously cultivated lands essential to the livelihood of an individual or a village.

The British also departed from Ottoman practice so as to prevent the cultivation of state lands without the Administration's permission. The Norwegian Refugee Council, in its "A Guide to Housing, Land and Property Law in the Gaza Strip," states:

> The Law of Land Transactions No. (39) of 1920 established new procedures, including the requirement to obtain the written consent of the Land Registration Director for any transaction concerning real estate, otherwise, the transaction will be considered null and void. Article 2 of the Palestine Order in Council of 1922 introduced a new type of land in the form of public land. This refers to all land under the supervision of the government of Palestine in accordance with treaties, agreements or inherited laws, as well as all land owned for the public interest, or other land. Other provisions in the 1922 Order in Council granted the High Commissioner the authority to act on all rights involving public land or any related rights.[65]

Under Turkish land law, anyone could convert *Mewat* land into *Miri* land by cultivating it, registering it, and paying its unimproved value. With the British Administration Smith notes that "the area of cultivated land was increased while the state's rights over the land were preserved."[66] The Land Ordnance promulgated in October 1920 aimed to regulate and demarcate state land. In the second ordinance of 1921, the *Mewat Land Ordinance*, the British administration attempted both to stop further encroachment on state lands and to make people register waste land that they already had reclaimed.

The ordinances did not satisfy the provision in Clause 6 of the Mandate to facilitate Jewish settlement on state lands. In these circumstances, this could only be fulfilled by issuing leases on large tracts of state lands to Zionists agencies, but the practical arrangements were tense with difficulties. One obstacle was to terminate long-term leases which were part of the fragmentary and incomplete system of land registration in Palestine, and affected state land as well as other land. Since the Administration could not lease a tract of land without knowing its exact size and boundaries, it was necessary to introduce the Land Ordinance in 1920 and the *Mewat* Lands Ordinance in 1921, to protect state land from further alienation.

A closer reading of the legislation of state lands in the Ottoman Land Laws would have shown that reclaimed *Mewat* land became *Miri* land (thus the state retained the right to resume possession) if the owners had abandoned it for three successive years.

The land system defined in the Ottoman legislation reflects the central government's economic interests. Under the Land Code, an individual who possess land must obtain a *kushan* [land deed] from a government official. Under the Land Code, permission to possess *Miri* land is given against a dual payment: a leasehold fee that is paid in advance at the time the *kushan* is given, and an annual tithe on the crops grown on the land.

1967

In the aftermath of the Six Day War, the debate in Israel, of what to do with the territories, was vivid. Some politicians suggested autonomy to the Palestinians while other supported the idea of quickly establish a Palestinian Arab entity—maybe even a state—in an enclave along the mountain ridge of the West Bank, north of Jerusalem. One of Israel's, if not the most, prominent generals,

Yigal Allon stated: "We have never held territory without settling it."[67] Yigal Allon's thinking was in line with the mainstream Zionist thought. The internal debate in Israel was characterized, both by voices in support of settling the land, as well as rejection of this approach. The Labor politician Arie Elav was one of the Israeli voices that acknowledged the existence of a Palestinian people as a fact. While it could be that Zionism's struggle with Arab nationalism accidently had fueled the Palestinian nation, Israel needed to declare that "we will never repress the rights of the Palestinians to national self—determination, and we are willing to help them establish a state."[68]

Besides them being rivals, or maybe simply because of that, there was a difference in reasoning about what do with the newly conquered areas, between Moshe Dayan and Yigal Allon (both considered mythological war heroes in Israel). Dayan didn't want Jewish settlers in the West Bank.[69] Yigal Allon, on the other hand, wanted the opposite. He never "forgave Ben Gurion for keeping us from retaking the Etzion bloc" at the end of the war of independence.[70]

However Israeli policy of settling the land, was not entirely a result of its governments' and leaders' willingness or idealism. Rather it was a consequence of activists, pulling in officers and officials sympathetic to its cause, with the intent of dragging the government after them. Activists would set policy and draw the map of the country themselves.[71]

When Israel Defence Forces (IDF) entered the West Bank in 1967, an area of 1,445,000 acres came under its jurisdiction.[72] This happened during a time, begun in the British mandatory period and continued under the Jordanians, of establishing order in land registration by determining and recording the various landowners in the registry. This formal process, which would have required many years to complete, was interrupted at a time when only 30 percent of the land in the West Bank had been registered. In *Geography and Politics in Israel since 1967*, Elisha Efrat explains that the areas included in the registration mainly covered the area north of the Jerusalem-Jericho, the Jordan Valley, Tulkarm and Qalqilya.[73] The registration stopped with the conquest of the area, as the Geneva Convention forbade changes to be instituted under a military government.

As mentioned above, there was no comprehensive registration of title based on land "settlement" in the West Bank—a process which includes cadastral surveying, measurement, initial boundary setting, quasi-judicial hearing, determination of objections, and finally registration. Since approximately two thirds of the non-urban land in the West Bank remained "unsettled," development was stalled.

Around the time of the conquest (following the Six Day War), in most of the West Bank it was possible under conditions of non-registration to consider as potential State land all land except: (a) land registered as private property and which can be proved to be such, (b) land cultivated for at least ten years, giving the farmer certain rights over it (The Law of Limitation made this even more stringent), and (c) land belonging to 1967 absentees managed under the abandoned property decree, and returnable in the condition it was in at the time of seizure, when the owners return.[74] At the same time, there is a military government with extensive powers regarding land which, in the absence of registration, operates on the basis of national and security needs and considerations. This often leads to legal confrontations between local residents and the Israeli authorities, and against the background of the confusion, many difficulties arise. Certainly, if land registration were completed for the whole West Bank it would be useful for both Israelis and Palestinians alike, and many unpleasant episodes related to the competition for land could be avoided.

In order to determine which lands were government owned in a practical and evidentiary manner, the IDF military commander exercised his authority to declare land which apparently has been abandoned or uncultivated, as state lands. Prior to issuing such declaration, however, a forty-five days' notice of his intention is published in the civilian coordination and communication centers, and notice is served on the leaders of the relevant village, giving objectors an opportunity to prove otherwise. Only after a very thorough examination of the state of cultivation of the land and confirmation that it had not been worked for a period even extending up to ten years, is the land declared state land.

In the areas where the registration was completed, there are accurate records of ownership, and the Israelis can operate easily only in connection with state land. The term covers all categories of land, except the land that is owned by local residents; these categories have all now the legal status of "land in direct Israeli ownership." Efrat argues that in other areas, the major part of the West Bank, no registration took place, and thus the ownership is not recorded. The Israeli government adopted a land policy based on the Ottoman land law which states:

> Empty land, such as mountains, rocky areas, rough terrain, pastures, which are not owned by anyone on the basis of a deed, and are not designated for the use of any city or village-dwellers, and are such a distance from cities or villages that a person's voice cannot be heard in the closest settlement [those areas] are known as dead land ... any person who needs such land can with the consent of the official, cultivate it, except that the absolute owner will be the Sultan.[75]

The essence of this law is that any land that is uncultivated or uncultivable, and is not recognized private land, is State land. In light of the fact that 60 percent of the land in the West Bank is not cultivable, a large proportion of it in the unregistered areas can be considered State land.

The old ideology of the Labour movement, which since pre-State had made agricultural policies as their main focus, began to apply this also in the West Bank. It became important to find fertile land to cultivate, which was a difficult task since much of the land is rocky and the little cultivable land was already exploited by the locals. As a result, it was a problem to obtain agricultural land for the settlements. It was solved by the government through declaring the land as belonging to absentees, and then leasing it to settlers, or using a policy in which the state seized land was deemed for use due to security purposes.

1979

Until 1979, the military commander founded Israeli settlements in the area by using military seizure orders, in accordance with his mandate to ensure security and public order. However, in 1979 the Israeli High Court of Justice ruled, in HCJ 390/79 *Dwikat v. State of Israel*,[76] that the security purpose cited for the establishment of Elon Moreh was only a secondary purpose, therefore the seizure of property for Elon Moreh's establishment was not in accordance with the military commander's mandate. Following the final ruling on the Elon Moreh case 1979, "Israel intensified its process of surveying, identifying and confiscating lands under Military Order (MO) 59. It identified an additional 1.5 million *dunum* (1 500 km2) of land in various categories—about 26 percent of the West Bank—that could still be confiscated in this manner."[77] And also, following the *Elon Moreh* decision, the Cabinet decided that all uncultivated rural land would be declared state land. The onus would be placed on individuals to prove their rights in the land. This could be done only by providing title deeds or by providing evidence attesting to both possession and cultivation of the land for a period of at least ten years.[78] According to the Ottoman Land Code, for the grantee to continue to hold some sort of property rights, the governing authority had to be paid taxes and tithes.

Even when land actually was registered in the Ottoman land registry offices, the verbal description of the parcel borders and other information frequently did not reflect the reality of the land in question. In addition to this, many peasants refrained from registering land transactions, fearing that such registration would attract the attention of tax collectors or be used as a mechanism for military conscription. Thus, the formal system of registration did not address the needs of those in possession of the land and only about 5 percent of the land in Palestine had been registered by the end of the Ottoman period.[79]

In other words, a title deed is not enough; the land not only had to be used, but also the taxes and fees had to be paid. If a person cultivated an area for ten consecutive years, he could apply for a title deed. But, if the land were abandoned at any time, even though he had cultivated it for a few years, he would lose his claim to ownership and the grant. Even if he could apply and did not, or did not pay the taxes or the tithes, the land would revert to the governing authority.

The *Elon Moreh* ruling was the point at which the state could have limited the High Court from intervening further in the settlement enterprise. In other words, if the Knesset had decided back then to limit the High Court from deciding certain issues related to the settlements, it would have been easier politically to "get away with it" than it is now when there are decades of court decisions regarding settlement issues. Since its ruling in the *Elon Moreh* case, the Supreme Court has not intervened in the steps taken by the government to gain control of West Bank land, and it has refrained from ruling on the legality of most of the substantive components of the declaration policy.

Benvenisti argues that, "since the issues of settlements and economic integration were so contentious within Israeli public opinion, the Court's stance would seem warranted." The problem was that only part of the concerned public enjoyed access to the parliament, the Israeli Knesset. The Court "could not—balance the inherent political inferiority of the Arab population by requiring the government to refer to the Knesset to receive a clearer mandate for its policies."[80]

Also, since the relevant criterion for adjunction would have been international law, any ruling against the government under the law of occupation (and any consequential clearer mandate from the Knesset) might have depicted Israel as a violator of international law, tainting the government's general claim of legitimacy under this law. In light of these considerations and facing a government that was committed to expanding the settlements, the Court carefully avoided a ruling on their legality.

What is the legal status of Jewish settlers and how did their presence change the legal framework of the West Bank's status? Even if the 1967 Levi Eshkol government's original intention was mostly just to hold on to the West Bank as a bargaining chip to achieve peace, around three months after the war, on September 1, 1967, the Arab League declared it would not negotiate land for peace at the Khartoum Conference. According to Alan Baker, former Foreign Ministry top legal adviser and Levy Report author, the main change on the Israeli side has been placing greater emphasis on the basic historical and legal rights of the Jews to the land according to the Balfour Declaration, the 1920 San Remo Declaration and other pre-state documents.

Following the High Court decision, "the government adopted the new policy that enabled it to seize land for its own needs based on a government decree and the Ottoman land law stipulating that the local proprietors, not the government, must prove ownership."[81] The Ottoman law provides that land between villages for which there is no deed belongs to the Sultan. As only a third of the West Bank was ever registered, the ownership of two thirds cannot be proven. This effectively meant that 64 per cent of the land in the West Bank became potentially confiscatable for the purpose of establishing new Jewish settlements.[82] As explained by geographer Efrat, the expropriation of land for military purposes was accomplished by its requisition for security reasons. Demilitarization of specific strongholds was transformed into civilian settlements.

In turn, on November 11, 1979, the Israeli government decided that future settlements would be established on land, deemed by the law of the area to be state managed land and not on land seized for military purposes.[83] The legal framework for this decision was found in the 1858 "Ottoman Land Law, still then in effect in the West Bank and which provided that any uncultivated land 'beyond shouting range' of the closest village or town was the sultan's property. The switch from expropriation of private land to its recategorization as state land gave the state substantial advantages in terms of the legal process."[84] It shifted the burden of proof regarding ownership of the land to the Palestinian claimant, who now needed to provide proof of possession, in order to exclude their land from being considered state land. According to Plia Albeck, former head of the Civil Department in the State Attorney's Office, by 1985 approximately 90 percent of the settlements were established on land that had been declared state land.

"As international law requires an occupying power to refrain from making any substantial changes in the status of occupied territory except for reasons of security, the concept of security was repeatedly addressed by the Court on various occasions in which it had to review the legality of civilian settlements in the West Bank."[85]

Today, in order to establish a settlement there is a need for a governmental decision in a similar manner for the establishment of settlements within Israel. After a decision is reached, the military commander sets the boundaries of the settlement within which the relevant council may operate.

Also in 1979, along with the growth of the Israeli population in the area, a need for a new legal framework to govern that population arose. In turn, the military commander enacted military orders, which allowed the creation of regional and local councils in the area.

The purpose of the orders was to allow, among other things, the military commander to enact regulations in the various councils, through which he can apply various Israeli special norms to the residents of the councils. The importance of this was to allow the Israeli resident of the area to maintain a uniform code of conduct for an Israeli citizen residing in Israel proper. The regional and local councils of the area are similar to the municipal councils in Israel proper, with necessary adjustments made to suit their presence in an area under belligerent occupation.

THE CATEGORIZATION OF PRESENT LAND OWNERSHIP IN THE WEST BANK

In turn, a need to identify property arose throughout Judea and Samaria since roughly two-thirds of the land was not registered. Accordingly, in the late 1970s through the early 1980s, a delimitation project of "state lands" began.[86] At the time, the project was headed by the then head of Civilian Affairs in the State Attorney's Office, attorney Plia Albeck.

As the years progressed, it was discovered that the delimitation of "state land" in certain areas was not exact. In turn, in 1999, the State Property Delimitation Team (more commonly known as the "Blue Line" Team) was founded and tasked with using the more exact modern day means available, to reapply past delimitations in the area.

Present ownership of land in the West Bank can be categorized in the following ways:

- Land privately owned by Arabs
- Land privately owned by Jews
- State land

Private Arab Land

Private Arab Land is land that can be proved to be private property. For land that was registered, the registration is unequivocal proof. For unregistered land, it is up to the claimant to prove his ownership. The problem, however, is that the only proof recognized by law is the "registration extract," which is issued upon completion of the registration process, and if the process is not completed, the land in the area was never registered! One possibility is to use other evidence such as entry in tax lists and recording in the Mukthar's ledgers. Most tax entries refer to ownership of land that is not taxable, or for which tax was paid on only a small part. The consequence is that if the entry shows that no tax was levied, doubt is cast upon the claim to the land because if it belonged to the claimant and he/she cultivated it and lived off it, or if he held on to it as material property, he would have had to pay taxes on it.

"Throughout much of the country's history, the Supreme Court's treatment of expropriation of private land has been characterized by extreme deference to the executive branch."[87] Courts in general, and supreme courts in particular, tend not to challenge the state, or its centers of power and legal ideology. The functioning of courts as institutions which support the hegemony of the state is a well-documented phenomenon.

Private Jewish Land

Private Jewish Land is Jewish-owned land in the West Bank which was legally acquired before 1948. The best known are the tracts in Hebron and the Etzion bloc. At that time land was also acquired by various bodies, the largest being the JNF. From 1967, permission to purchase land in the West Bank has been given to Jews, first to public institutions like the JNF, and then, since 1979, to private individuals.

Efrat tells us that unlike the policy within pre-1967 Israel, the situation on the West Bank is quite different. The rest of the land that the settlers need in order to develop the infrastructure such as paved roads, public use, and industrial land use, is not private land, but rather State land or private Arab land legally appropriated for public purposes—"the public being the Jewish population which since 1972 has been legally recognized as part of the West Bank population. It appears that the amount of private Jewish land in the West Bank is very small,"[88] for there is both a financial and political risk in such purchases. However, private Jewish land exists. This is evident in the studies and observations made by Baruch Kimmerling. In the West Bank a national committee was established for the purchase of Arab lands which were liable to be sold to Jews.[89] Thus, during the seventies, Jordan's religious leaders declared that anyone selling his land to Israelis is a traitor to Islam and the Arab nation. Consequently, the General Manager of the JNF was forced to acknowledge that "since the beginning of the public debate over land purchases in Judea and Samaria, the supply of lands for sale has been reduced."[90]

Purchases of land by private entrepreneurs were permitted in cases which the Israel Land Authority could not purchase it or was not in interested in purchasing it.

Another source for the confirmation of private Jewish land in the West Bank is from the Palestinian negotiation team.[91] It was revealed in the so-called "Palestine Papers" that were leaked by Al Jazeera. In those papers there was "a draft memorandum to Palestinian Negotiating Team that discusses options for dealing with property claims of Jews within the West Bank acquired before the beginning of the occupation, covering Ottoman and British periods, Jordanian Rule of the West Bank and Egyptian rule of Gaza."[92] The purpose of the memo was to outline options for dealing with property claims of Jews within the West Bank acquired before 1967. It is declared that "Jews who lived in and/or owned property" and "who were subsequently displaced and/or dispossessed of their property are entitled to remedies for their losses under international law. They are in fact in a very similar position to that of Palestinians who were displaced and dispossessed in what became Israel."[93]

> Jews who were habitually resident before 1948 in the areas that became the [Occupied Palestinian Territory] OPT enjoy a right of return. It should be noted that the right of return extends not only to those persons who held the nationality of the prior sovereign, but also to persons who had a substantial connection to the prior state and who, therefore, were entitled to its nationality. The right also extends to the descendants of such Jews.
>
> As of 1948, there were 500,000 to 600,000 Jews in Palestine. Most of them were not nationals of Palestine. Of the 400,000 or so Jews who immigrated to Palestine between the two World Wars, 100,000 were naturalized. So, probably fewer than half of pre-1948 Jews were nationals, but most were probably permanent residents. According to international law, such Jewish Palestinian nationals or permanent residents have a right of residency in the future Palestinian state if they were residents of the areas that became Gaza and the [West Bank] WB.[94]

For instance, there

> was land located on Mount Scopus, which was purchased from a British national in 1916. Boris Goldberg, a member of Lovers of Zion, paid for the land and took title in his name. He gifted the land to the JNF, which gave a 999-year lease to Hebrew University. Additional land was purchased on Mount Scopus from Raghib al-Nashashibi, Mayor of Jerusalem, and was used for the Hebrew University. Hadassah Hospital was also built on land purchased on Mount Scopus.
>
> During the British mandate, most land purchases were concluded by the JNF, the [The Palestine Land Development Com-

> pany] PLDC, and the [Palestine Jewish Colonization Association] PJCA.
>
> Land purchased by the PLDC was transferred to the JNF. The JNF in turn leased (but did not sell) land to individual Jews. Thus, any Jew who lived on JNF land before 1948 would not have held title.
>
> In the case of the PJCA, it sold some of its land to individual Jews under long instalment plans or granted long-term leases. Some PJCA land may have never been sold and thus remained in its ownership, some may have been leased and thus remained in its ownership, and some may have been sold but the instalment payments not made in full.[95]

Other examples of private lands were:

- By 1946, the JNF acquired 72,300 dunums in the Gaza district, which encompassed more than present-day Gaza.
- In 1930, a Jewish farmer from Rehovot, Tuvia Miller, bought 262 dunums of land in Dayr al-Balah in the Gaza sub-district. Miller eventually sold his land to the JNF in the early 1940s. The JNF then allowed settlers from the religious Ha-Poel ha-Mizrahi movement to build the kibbutz of Kfar Darom on the land in October 1946. They abandoned the kibbutz in June 1948.
- Purchase of 4,048 dunums in Huj (Gaza sub-district) in 1935. The Palestine Partition Commission reported that, by 1938, 3,300 dunums in Gaza were owned by Jews.
- In 1941, 6,373 dunums were purchased by the JNF around Gaza City. The government of Palestine estimated a population of 3,540 Jews in the Gaza sub-district at the end of 1946. Information has not been found on the circumstances under which these Jews departed from Gaza in 1948.[96]

The Palestine Papers released by Al Jazeera reveals Palestinian negotiator's own estimate of dunums owned by Jews by 1948 in the West Bank.

- There were Jewish settlements north of Jerusalem called Atarot and Neve Yaakov, which were evacuated in 1948.
- A settlement called Bet Haarava, and Palestine Potash, Ltd., both located at the northern end of the Dead Sea, were situated on *miri* land leased by the government of Palestine and were evacuated in 1948.
- During the 1920s and 1930s, individual Jews and two Jewish-owned realty companies, Zikhron David and El Hahar, bought land in the hills around Hebron. The JNF began purchasing land around Hebron in 1940. It acquired about 8,400 dunums by 1947, some of which was purchased from individual Jews and from Zikhron David and El Hahar. The settlements established on this land were called Kfar Etzion, Masuot Yitzhak, Ein Tzurim and Revadim.
- Some 16,000 dunums of land were purchased by Jews before 1948 in the Etzion Bloc and Beit Hadassah.
- Land were bought near Jericho and present-day Maale Adumim. The funding in urban areas usually came from state coffers, while the purchase of agricultural land was paid for by the JNF.
- During the British mandate, the government of Palestine leased *miri* land on a long-term basis (50 or 100 years) to Jewish settlement organisations.
- By 1948, the concentrations of lands owned by Jews were in the old Jewish quarters of Jerusalem and Hebron, on the periphery of Jerusalem, and in the Tul-Karem region and the Gaza Strip.
- Apparently, 80% of Har Homa land is Jewish land purchased in the forties and before.[97]

Private Christian Land

Jerusalem is the declared eternal capital of one country, Israel, as well as that of Palestine. It is a city loved so intensely that it has driven—and continues to drive—some people insane. The answer, then, to the question of who owns Jerusalem: It is complicated. The issue of land ownership in the Holy City is not about Jews versus Arabs, the State of Israel versus the Palestinian Authority, or even Judaism versus Islam. Rather, the issue is about the residents of Jerusalem versus the legacy of history, or more specifically, the Christian churches and, lately, a few very astute—some might say rapacious—private investors.

> Much of the current population of Jerusalem is living on land that is owned by various Christian church denominations. While part of the Baka neighborhood and French Square belongs to the Franciscan order, and some of the Mount of Olives is owned by the Russian Orthodox Church, the lion's share—more than 60%—of church holdings in Jerusalem belong to the Greek Orthodox Patriarchate, including Rehavia, Talbiyeh, much of Katamon and Rassco, parts of Givat Ram, all of Nayot, as well as Liberty Bell Park, the Valley of the Cross, the area between the Yemin Moshe neighborhood and the King David Hotel, a portion of Keren Hayesod Street, part of the Mamilla Mall, as well as part of the land on which sit the Israel Museum, the Prime Minister's Residence, the President's Residence, the Knesset Building, the Chief Rabbinate and the Great Synagogue, among others.
>
> The invention and development of railroads and steamships made travel to the Holy Land much easier, especially from Europe. The second was political: Egypt invaded the Holy Land in 1832 and unceremoniously grabbed it away from the Ottomans.
>
> Anticipating tens of thousands of Christians coming on pilgrimage to the Holy Land—enabled by railroads, steamships and the now more liberal policies of the Ottoman government—these

> Christian groups began buying not only small parcels of land within the walled city, but also large swaths of land outside the walls. These groups included, among others, the Anglican Church of England, the Lutheran Church of Germany, the Young Men's Christian Association (YMCA) from the US, as well as the Greek Orthodox Church, which saw itself as the successor of the Byzantines and was thus particularly driven to "regain" the Holy Land. From 1860 onwards, the same steamships that were bringing Christians were also bringing significant numbers of Jews, who began to build residential neighborhoods outside the Old City walls.[98]

Churches began to lease portions of their enormous land holdings for the construction of residential and commercial buildings, not only in Jerusalem but throughout Ottoman and later British Mandate Palestine. The Greek Orthodox Church in particular found itself in rather dire financial straits in the 1920s. Prohibited by church rules against selling its land outright, it instead leased most of its land to the Keren Kayemeth LeIsrael-Jewish National Fund and received a sizable payment upfront in exchange for the Jewish community's right to use the land on a long-term basis.[99]

> In 1952 the Patriarchate signed an agreement deal that left it with formal ownership of its land in Jerusalem, with the KKL-JNF obtaining all rights to use and develop the land through a long-term lease of 99 years, valid until the year 2051. The agreement furthermore entitled the KKL-JNF to sublease the land to private investors and developers, who immediately began constructing various kinds of buildings, including tens of thousands of residential units.
>
> The agreement also clearly stipulated that the land—along with the properties built on the land—would completely revert to the Greek Orthodox Patriarchate when the lease runs out in 2051. The original terms allowed the KKL-JNF to sublease the land to various developers, which built on the properties—including thousands of homes. But the original lease stated that the Patri-

archate would once again receive the full and sole rights to the properties when the lease runs out in 2051.

State Land

State Land includes most of the territory of the West Bank under direct Israeli control and is classified in the following formal categories, according to Efrat's *Geography and Politics in Israel*:

> Absentee land- land or other property to citizens of the West Bank who left after 1967. This land is managed under the Abandoned Property Order by the Official in Charge of Absentee Property in the Israel Land Authority. For most, this land is left unutilized and no changes are instituted in it (retaining the status quo in case the owner returns) and in others the Official has leased it to private individuals to cultivate, but the absentee can recover it upon his return. For example: a large proportion of the land in the Jordan Valley is absentee land leased to the settlements there, and the rental fee is credited to the original proprietor.[100]

Military Order 58, *Order Concerning Absentee Property* (Private Property) (23 July 1967) "property whose legal owner, or whoever is granted the power to control it by law, left the area prior to 7 June 1967 or subsequently" is declared 'abandoned' or 'absentee' property."[101]

The Area Commander may appoint a "Custodian of Absentee Property" to take control of all matters related to the property in question, including the authority to rent or sell it as he sees fit. The "Custodian" may also appoint other officials to oversee the property. To him are transferred all rights previously vested in the owner. Military Order 58 warns that anyone controlling property belonging to an "absentee" owner must declare this property as such or risk punishment. If the owner returns to the area legally, the property may be restored to him (after deduction of an administrative fee) if he can credibly establish his property rights.

According to Article 5 of this Military Order: "any transaction carried out in good faith between the Custodian of Absentee Property and any other person, concerning property which the Custodian believed when he entered into the transaction to be Absentee Property, will not be void and will continue to be valid even if it is subsequently proved that the property was not at that time Absentee Property."[102]

Another Military Order of interest is 150, *Order Concerning Absentee Property* of October 23, 1967. This Military Order widens the scope of MO 58 by defining "abandoned property" as that which is owned or controlled by a resident of a "hostile" country. It also establishes provisions for the transfer of assets and control of any businesses owned by an "absentee." (MO 150 was amended by the separate MO 358 in 1969).

Theoretically and legally, the Custodian is entrusted with protecting the property and assets of absentees until they return to reclaim their rights. Palestinians who have returned to the area under processes including family reunification and have tried to reclaim their lands have been frustrated by the good faith provision, which is virtually impossible to overrule. The merger of the different "Custodian" functions into a joint "Custodian of Government and Abandoned Property in Judea and Samaria" has facilitated Israel's declarations of "abandoned" land as State land.

- Registered State land—is land that is registered in the name of the King of Jordan or the British High Commissioner who preceded him. The Military Government acts as temporary authority but in practice deals with it as it does with Israeli State land and leases it to Jewish settlers.

  Many Jewish settlements are located on land belonging to this category, with leases for 49 or 99 years with options to extend. This was done possible due to the interpretation of Israel's status in the West Bank as the original ruler that had returned. If Israel would have had annexed the region and become the legal heir of the Jordanian authorities, the land would become its absolute property.

- Land expropriated for public needs—land laws in many countries allow the authorities to expropriate land for the needs of the public. The land is primarily aimed for infrastructure.
- Areas closed for military purposes—these areas are closed by the Military Government on the basis of an 'Occupation Order', which are intended for training, shooting ranges, security zones etc. The land in question remains the property of the local owners.
- Land confiscated for military purposes—land that is privately owned by Arab residents, which is taken over by the Military Government on the grounds that it is vital for military purposes. According to Efrat, there is no real dispossession, for the registered ownership is preserved and the Military Government pays the landowner a fee in compensation.
- Land without owners—is land in which the local people cannot prove legal ownership. It becomes State land.[103]

The total numbers regarding acres on the land differ depending on what kind of category the land falls in under. Jewish owned land in the West Bank, acquired before 1948 and after 1967, is about 17 500 acres while Absentee is about 107 500 acres. Registered State Land amounts to 175 000 acres which is about one- eight of all land in the West Bank. Land expropriated for public needs is estimated at about 25 000 acres.

The two most widely used official means for taking over lands in the West Bank for the settlements, including for agriculture, arc military seizure orders and declaration of state lands.

Military Order 59, *Order Concerning State Property*, enacted July 31, 1967, "proved to be one of the most far-reaching measures in providing Israel with legal cover to take over vast areas of Palestinian land in the Territories. . . . MO [Military Order] 59 defines 'State property' as any property belonging to a 'hostile state' before

7 June 1967, or any property belonging to an arbitration body connected to a hostile state."[104]

Besides the official measures Israel has used to take over lands in the West Bank, the state has also, over the course of decades, encouraged settler takeovers of additional areas, both public (state) lands and private Palestinian lands. Hence, a large part of Israeli agriculture in the West Bank is a result of patently illegal activity, both according to international law and according to Israeli military and civil law.[105]

According to the report written by BADIL and COHRE, Israel employed its unique interpretations of Ottoman and Jordanian law to redefine requirements for the registration of particular types of land, and then proceeded to confiscate such lands when Palestinians were unable to, or were prevented from, meeting the new requirements.[106]

Paralleling the Jewish aspirations to control the land in the West Bank, there is action on the part of the Arab population which can be explained according to following:

- unsupervised extension of village areas by scattered buildings
- construction in isolated spots unconnected with villages
- resumption of cultivation of abandoned fields

This activity has political encouragement and outside financing, as a reaction to the policy of the military government and to Jewish interest in the West Bank.[107] The Arabs occupy State land, and land that may potentially become State land, and entrench themselves on it by establishing facts on the ground, hoping to expand their future subsistence area, which is reduced with every new Jewish settlement founded. By building around existing villages in a wide circle aimed at physically extending the village area (and also outside the villages on State land where they put up provisional structures) and undertake some cultivation they seek to demonstrate their connection with that tract of the land.

In light of what was seen as increasing penetration of the Arab inhabitants into State land, action was taken in 1981 to prevent and reduce such actions. This was done by seizing State land, in order to consolidate State ownership. The aims were among others:

- to secure the boundaries of the Jewish settlements and adjacent State land
- to protect land reserves for future settlement, or for developing industrial areas
- to guarantee physical continuity between the Jewish settlements, in the long term and at small cost.[108]

This was enforced by the JNF, and it employed means to carry out the above mentioned aims for the creation of land that could be used for agriculture. Among the methods that were being used included development of pastures, afforestation, parks for residents and tourists, and archeological excavations. Naturally these activities involved more than the physical occupation of the land since they necessitate investment in the short term as an incentive for the development of physical presence in these areas.

A recent released study, "Measure for Measure 2018: An Index of Judicial Parity,"[109] reported by the *Jewish News Syndicate*, analyzed petitions filed in Israel's Supreme Court against illegal construction in the West Bank revealed preferential treatment given to leftist, and pro-Palestinian Groups against Jewish settlements. Almost all of the petitions were based on identical points of law. The study showed "that the state was allowed an average of 18.5 days to file a preliminary response" over petitions filed by leftist groups against Jewish construction. In comparison, "petitions by Israeli nationalist groups against Arab construction that number soared to 30.5 days. . . . Jewish petitioners waited an average of three months longer for a first hearing."[110]

Pro-Palestinian groups were found to receive seven times more interim orders and temporary injunctions than pro-Zionist groups.

Additionally, "21 percent of Israeli nationalist cases earned the presence of the chief justice presiding, whereas the judge presided in 58 percent of pro-Palestinian cases."[111]

NOTES

1. Council of the League of Nations, "The Palestine Mandate," London, July 24, 1922, Article 6, http://avalon.law.yale.edu/20th_century/palmanda.asp (accessed May 29, 2018).

2. Council of the League of Nations, "The Palestine Mandate," Article 6 states "The Administration of Palestine, while ensuring that the rights and position of other sections of the population are not prejudiced, shall facilitate Jewish immigration under suitable conditions and shall encourage, in co-operation with the Jewish agency referred to in Article 4, close settlement by Jews on the land, including State lands and waste lands not required for public purposes." In a report by Kerem Navot, the Executive Summary, of Article 6 notes that, "The Zionist ideal of Jewish agriculture" also became a central component in the West Bank (Judea and Samaria)

> by which the settlement movement (with the overt or tacit approval and direct or indirect support of the state) staked a claim to and consolidated control over large areas of the West Bank. The first Israeli West-Bank settlers viewed agriculture as a means of solidifying Jewish settlement in the West Bank for three main reasons: *Ideological/ religious*—Agricultural activity bolstered the claim that the Israeli settlement in Judea and Samaria constituted a return to the "Land of the Fathers" and to the times when agriculture was a source of livelihood for the ancient Jewish communities in the region; *Economic*—Agriculture was considered an economic base on which the first settlements could subsist and develop, though with time, agriculture became less significant as a source of livelihood for the settler population; and *Territorial*—Agricultural activity was a key means with which to expand the territory of the nascent settlement enterprise. (6)

For further reading see, Kerem Navot, "Israeli Settler Agriculture as a Means of Land Takeover in the West Bank," August 2013. http://rhr.org.il/heb/wp-content/uploads/Kerem-Navot.pdf (May 26, 2018.

3. Barbara J. Smith, *The Roots of Separatism in Palestine: British Economic Policy, 1920–1929* (Syracuse, NY: Syracuse University Press, 1993), 86.

4. Council of the League of Nations, "The Palestine Mandate."

5. Smith, *Roots of Separatism*, 89.

6. Alexandre (Sandy) Kedar, "The Legal Transformation of Ethnic Geography: Israeli Law and the Palestinian Landholder, 1948–1967," *New York Univer-*

sity Journal of International Law and Politics 33, no. 4 (Summer 2001): 923–1000 at page. 940.

7. Jewish Agency, "Modern Zionist Aliyot to Israel, About the waves of Jewish immigration to Israel (Aliot) 1882–1948," November 13, 2014, http://www.jewishagency.org/historical-aliyah/content/28841 (accessed July 2, 2018). See also Jewish Agency, "Historical Aliyah," December 18, 2005, http://www.jewishagency.org/historical-aliyah/content/23440 (accessed July 2, 2018).

8. Yifat Holzman-Gazit, *Land Expropriation in Israel: Law Culture and Society* (Aldershot, UK: Ashgate, 2007), 57.

9. The Workers' Movement, Tnuat Ha'avoah, was the dominant political group during the years preceding the establishment of the State. For further reading see Kedar, "Legal Transformation," 940.

10. Leviticus 25:23, New American Standard Bible (ASV), available online at http://biblehub.com/leviticus/25-23.htm (accessed May 29, 2018).

11. Kedar, "Legal Transformation," 941.

12. Leviticus 25:10-13, AVS.

13. Holzman-Gazit, *Land Expropriation in Israel* (2007), 59.

14. Kedar, "Legal Transformation," page 943.

15. Onit Arfa, "Who REALLY owns the Land of Israel?" *Jewish Journal*, December 31, 2013, http://jewishjournal.com/opinion/marty_kaplan/125677/who-really-owns-the-land-of-israel/ (accessed May 24, 2018).

16. Arfa, "Who REALLY owns the Land of Israel?"

17. Arfa, "Who REALLY owns the Land of Israel?"

18. Arfa, "Who REALLY owns the Land of Israel?"

19. Arfa, "Who REALLY owns the Land of Israel?"

20. Holzman-Gazit, *Land Expropriation in Israel* (2007), 103.

21. Holzman-Gazit, *Land Expropriation in Israel* (2007), 103.

22. Holzman-Gazit, *Land Expropriation in Israel* (2007), 105.

23. Holzman-Gazit, *Land Expropriation in Israel* (2007), 24.

24. *New Perspectives on Property and Land in the Middle East*, ed. Roger Owen (Cambridge, MA: Center for Middle Eastern Studies, Harvard University Press, 2000), 26.

25. *New Perspectives*, ed. Owen, 26.

26. *New Perspectives*, ed. Owen, 32.

27. *New Perspectives*, ed. Owen, 32.

28. Israel, Ministry of Foreign Affairs, "The Judiciary: The Court System," 2013, http://www.mfa.gov.il/mfa/aboutisrael/state/democracy/pages/the%20judiciary-%20the%20court%20system.aspx (accessed May 26, 2018).

29. Eyal Benvenisti, *The International Law of Occupation*, new ed. (Princeton, NJ: Princeton University Press, 2004), 118.

30. Benvenisti, *International Law of Occupation*, 119.

31. Benvenisti, *International Law of Occupation*, 122.

32. Ibid.,1. For further reading see, Israel, Ministry of Foreign Affairs, "Planning and Building Law- 1965" http://mfa.gov.il/MFA/PressRoom/1998/Pages/Planning%20and%20Building%20Law-%201965.aspx(accessed June 10, 2018)

& Israel, Ministry of Justice, "Expropriations Objections Committee" http://www.justice.gov.il/En/Units/ExpropriationsObjectionsCommittee/Pages/default.aspx (accessed June 10, 2018).

33. United Nations, Information System on the Question of Palestine (UNISPAL), "Palestine: The Palestine Order in Council," August 10, 1922, https://unispal.un.org/DPA/DPR/unispal.nsf/0/
C7AAE196F41AA055052565F50054E656 (accessed May 27, 2018)

34. Kedar, "Legal Transformation," 923-1000, page 937.

35. BADIL Staff, "Land Ownership in Palestine/Israel (1920-2000)," *Stocktaking and Perspectives* 5 (Spring 2002), http://www.badil.org/en/component/k2/item/1055-land-ownership-in-palestine.html (accessed May 25, 2018).

36. The District Court in Beersheba Civil Case File Nos. 7161/06, 7275/06, 7276/06 1114/07, 1115/07, 5278/08, *El Uqbi vs The State of Israel.* District Court Judgement of March 15, 2012.

37. District Court in Beersheba Civil Case File Nos. 7161/06, 7275/06, 7276/06 1114/07, 1115/07, 5278/08.

38. District Court in Beersheba Civil Case File Nos. 7161/06, 7275/06, 7276/06 1114/07, 1115/07, 5278/08.

39. Havatzelet Yahel, *Land Disputes Between the Negev Bedouin and Israel, Israel Studies* 11, no. 2 (2006): 11–12, http://weblaw.haifa.ac.il/he/Faculty/Kedar/lecdb/landregime/112.pdf (accessed May 25, 2018). This is contested by Oren Yiftachel, former co-chairman of B'tselem, who argue that Israel has ignored the more inconvenient clauses of Ottoman law and replaced them with a Mandatory ordinance, which was meant to demarcate public lands in a completely different context. See Yiftachel, "The Law That Exposes Israel's True Colonialist Colors," *Haaretz. Opinoin*, December 14, 2016, http://www.haaretz.com/opinion/.premium-1.758794?=&ts=_1500979116702 (accessed May 27, 2018).

40. Kedar, "Legal Transformation," 923-1000.

41. Ya'akov Meron, "Waste Land (Mewat) in Judea and Samaria," *ICLR: International and Comparative Law Review* 4, no. 1 (Spring 1981): 3, http://lawdigitalcommons.bc.edu/iclr/vol4/iss1/2 (accessed May 26, 2018).

42. Smith, *Roots of Separatism*, 90.

43. Israel, *Al-Uqbi et al. v. State of Israel*, case [C.A.] 4220/12, Supreme Court Judgement of May 14, 2015.

44. Israel, *Al-Uqbi et al. v. State of Israel.*

45. An English translation by F. Ongley of the Ottoman Land Code is available at http://archive.org/stream/ottomanlandcode00turkuoft/ottomanlandcode00turkuoft_djvu.txt (accessed June 11, 2018).

46. Kedar, "Legal Transformation," 970.

47. Kedar, "Legal Transformation," 970.

48. B'Tselem, "Under the Guise of Legality: Israel's Declarations of State Land in the West Bank," report, February 2012, 23, https://www.btselem.org/download/201203_under_the_guise_of_legality_eng.pdf (accessed May 25, 2018. In the report, the combination of acquired rights under Section 20 or under

Section 78 of the Ottoman Land Code along with Section 22 of the Prescription Law, is omitted.

49. Centre on Housing *The Ottoman Land Code*, trans. Frank Ongley (London: Forgotten Books, 2015), 45Rights and Evictions (CHOHRE), and BADIL Resource Center for Palestinian Residency and Refugees Rights, "Ruling Palestine: A History of the Legally Sanctioned Jewish-Israeli Seizure of Land and Housing in Palestine," May 2005, http://www.badil.org/phocadownloadpap/Badil_docs/publications/Ruling%20Palestine.pdf (accessed May 25, 2018).

50. Meron, "Waste Land (Mewat) in Judea and Samaria," 4.

51. Meron, "Waste Land (Mewat) in Judea and Samaria," 5.

52. Meron, "Waste Land (Mewat) in Judea and Samaria," 4–5.

53. I Meron, "Waste Land (Mewat) in Judea and Samaria," 29–30.

54. Smith, *Roots of Separatism*, 99.

55. B'Tselem, "Under the Guise of Legality," 22.

56. CHOHRE and BADIL, "Ruling Palestine," 59.

57. Meron, "Waste Land (Mewat) in Judea and Samaria," 32.

58. B'Tselem, "Under the Guise of Legality," 23.

59. Israel, Office of the Deputy Attorney General (International Law), Appeal on the judgment of the Beer Sheva District Court in Civil Case File Nos. 716/06, 7275/06,7276/06, 1114/07,1115/07, 5278/08. Israel, *Al-Uqbi et al. v. State of Israel*, case [C.A.] 4220/12, Supreme Court Judgement of May 14, 2015.

60. Meron, "Waste Land (Mewat) in Judea and Samaria," 10-11.

61. Smith, *Roots of Separatism*, 52.

62. Martin Bunton, "Demarcating the British Colonial State: Land Settlement in the Palestine *Jiftlik* Villages of Sajad and Qazaza," in *New Perspectives on Property and Land in the Middle East*, ed. Roger Owen (Cambridge, MA: Center for Middle Eastern Studies, Harvard University Press, 2000), 122.

63. Smith, *Roots of Separatism*, 98.

64. Smith, *Roots of Separatism*, 99–100.

65. Norwegian Refugee Council, and Jehad Arafat, Mona Abed Al Aziz, Fatma Al Sharif, and Yaser Al Manama, "A Guide to Housing, Land and Property Law in the Gaza Strip," ed. Elisabeth Koek, Martin Clutterbuck, and Alon Margalit, October 2015. https://www.nrc.no/globalassets/pdf/reports/a-guide-to-housing-land-and-property-law-in-the-gaza-strip-october-2015.pdf (accessed May 26, 2018).

66. Smith, *Roots of Separatism*, 98–99.

67. Gershom Gorenberg, *The Accidental Empire: Israel and the Birth of the Settlements, 1967–1977* (New York: Holt Paperbacks; 2007), 51.

68. Gorenberg, *Accidental Empire*, 175.

69. Gorenberg, *Accidental Empire*, 105.

70. Gorenberg, *Accidental Empire*, 105.

71. Gorenberg, *Accidental Empire*, 71.

72. Elisha Efrat, *Geography and Politics in Israel since 1967* (New York: Routledge, 2005), 59.

73. Efrat, *Geography and Politics in Israel since 1967*, 60.

74. Efrat, *Geography and Politics in Israel since 1967*, 61.

75. See *The Ottoman Land Code*, trans. Frank Ongley (London: Forgotten Books, 2015).

76. See Israel, High Court of Justice, *Duweikat et al. v. Government of Israel et al*. Judgment. HCJ 390/79, October 22, 1979, http://www.hamoked.org/Document.aspx?dID=1670 (accessed May 25, 2018); and High Court of Justice, *'Izzat Muhammad Mustafa Duweikat et 16 al. v. 1. Government of Israel 2. Minister of Defense 3. Military Commander for the Judea and Samaria Area 4. Nablus District Military Commander 5. Felix Menahem 6. Shvut Avraham*, Case HCJ 390/79, September 6-October 22, 1979, http://www.hamoked.org/files/2010/1670_eng.pdf (accessed May 25, 2018).

77. CHOHRE and BADIL, "Ruling Palestine," 90; emphasis mine. A *dunum* equates today to approximately 1,000 square meters of land.

78. The requirement of possession and cultivation for ten years is based on Article 78 of the Ottoman Land Law that was still in force when the IDF entered the area in 1967. This provision states that if a person has been in possession of and has cultivated miri land for a period of ten years, he or she is entitled to demand that the land be registered in his or her name (Ari Briggs, "Beware Ottoman Land Law!" *Jerusalem Post*, July 30, 2015, http://www.jpost.com/Opinion/Beware-Ottoman-land-law-410708 [accessed May 31, 2018]).

79. Kedar, "Legal Transformation," 923–1000.

80. Benvenisti, *International Law of Occupation*, 123.

81. Efrat, *Geography and Politics in Israel*, 51.

82. Efrat, *Geography and Politics in Israel*, 52.

83. Regional and Local Councils of Judea & Samaria, June 22, 2017, Legal Advisor of Judea and Samaria, http://www.law.idf.il/163-6731-en/Patzar.aspx?SearchText=state land (accessed May 26, 2018).

84. Holzman-Gazit, *Land Expropriation in Israel* (2007), 133.

85. Holzman-Gazit, *Land Expropriation in Israel* (2007), 134.

86. State Property Delimitation Team, הפרקליטות הצבאית, http://www.law.idf.il/163-6731-en/Patzar.aspx?SearchText=state land.

87. Holzman-Gazit, *Land Expropriation in Israel* (2007), 1.

88. Efrat, *Geography and Politics in Israel*, 64.

89. Baruch Kimmerling, *Zionism and Territory: The Socio-Territorial Dimensions of Zionist Politics* (Berkeley: Institute of International Studies, University of California, 1983), 164.

90. Kimmerling, *Zionism and Territory*, 164.

91. Al Jazeera, "The Palestine Papers: NSU Draft Memo Re: Rights of Jews Within the OPT Acquired pre-1967," September 2008, http://www.ajtransparency.com/en/projects/thepalestinepapers/20121820352521 8283.html (accessed May 24, 2018).

92. Al Jazeera, "The Palestine Papers."

93. Al Jazeera, "The Palestine Papers."

94. Al Jazeera, "The Palestine Papers."

95. Al Jazeera, "The Palestine Papers."

96. Al Jazeera, "The Palestine Papers."

97. Al Jazeera, "The Palestine Papers."

98. Carl Hoffman, "Who Owns the Holy City? The Jerusalem Question," *Jerusalem Post*, May 13, 2017, http://www.jpost.com/In-Jerusalem/Who-owns-the-Holy-City-484366 (accessed May 25, 2018).

99. Hoffman, "Who Owns the Holy City?"

100. Efrat, *Geography and Politics in Israel*, 64.

101. CHOHRE and BADIL, "Ruling Palestine," 86.

102. CHOHRE and BADIL, "Ruling Palestine," 85.

103. Efrat, *Geography and Politics in Israel,* 64.

104. CHOHRE and BADIL, "Ruling Palestine," 89.

105. Kerem Navot, "Israeli Settler Agriculture as a Means of Land Takeover in the West Bank," August 2013, http://rhr.org.il/heb/wp-content/uploads/Kerem-Navot.pdf (May 26, 2018).

106. CHOHRE and BADIL, "Ruling Palestine," 89.

107. Efrat, *Geography and Politics in Israel*, 65; Bassam Tawil, "The Real Illegal Settlements," *Gatestone Institute*, December 5, 2016, https://www.gatestoneinstitute.org/9490/illegal-settlements (accessed May 27, 2018).

108. Efrat, *Geography and Politics in Israel*, 65.

109. Jewish New Syndicate, "Study Finds Major Israeli Supreme Court Procedural Discrimination in Favor of Pro-Palestinian Plaintiffs," June 28, 2018, https://www.jns.org/study-finds-major-israeli-supreme-court-procedural-discrimination-in-favor-of-pro-palestinian-plaintiffs/ (accessed July 3, 2018).

110. Jewish New Syndicate, "Study Finds Major Israeli Supreme Court Procedural Discrimination in Favor of Pro-Palestinian Plaintiffs," June 28, 2018, https://www.jns.org/study-finds-major-israeli-supreme-court-procedural-discrimination-in-favor-of-pro-palestinian-plaintiffs/ (accessed July 3, 2018).

111. Jewish New Syndicate, "Study."

Chapter Two

The Land Laws: Different Takings and Approaches

Legal systems differ in their approach to the enforcement of international law in their domestic courts. The approach of English law is based on a distinction between two sources of international law. Norms of customary international law are regarded as part and parcel of the common law of the realm, and as such they are applied in domestic courts, unless a law is inconsistent with an act of parliament. Norms of conventional law do not automatically become part of the domestic law of the land. Courts do not enforce them unless they have been incorporated into domestic law by an act of parliament. The Supreme Court of Israel adopted this approach to international law long before the acquisition of the West Bank.

As mentioned earlier, no comprehensive registration of land ownership existed for the West Bank in 1967. Only one-third of the land had been registered. The practical result was that the status of two-thirds of West Bank land that was not registered in the land registry prior to June 1967 remained unclear. This unregistered land did not have maps and did not describe the precise boundaries of each lot.

Quite soon after the Six Day War (June 5-10, 1967), a military order was promulgated dealing with state land.[1] Under this use order the Custodian of Government Property appointed by the military governor is empowered to take possession of government property and regulate its use.

> In the absence of registration in the land registry, and since most Palestinians do not have *kushans* [title deeds], Israel subsequently claimed that much of the unregistered land was government property and declared it as state land. . . . The declarations of state land conducted by Israel deviate from the practice established during the British Mandate and Jordanian periods. Under both the Mandate government and Jordanian rule, the authorities did not actively seek out land that could be deemed state land.[2]

To nationalize land, free of competing, private Palestinian rights, Israel employed several methods. Most prominently, it massively declared land as "no man's land,"[3] which is, by law, State land. Land which was not in anyone's possession or being cultivated qualified for State land designation (which included Mêwat land). According to Ronit Levine Schnur, Israel—backed by the Supreme Court—ignored any claims for collective rights of communities, villages, or the Palestinian people as a whole. Only specific claims were considered for review. If claims were filed, in most of the cases Palestinians were unable to meet the high standard of proof.

When Palestinians objected to state land declarations, the primary question was whether they were able to prove their individual right under Article 78 of the Ottoman Land Code, 1858 (OLC).[4] To defeat a declaration, a claimant had to prove that he had cultivated the land for at least ten consecutive years without interruption prior to the declaration. And it would become even more difficult with

> the enactment of the Law of the Limitation in 1958, which introduced several changes that were seemingly technical, but which had far- reaching implications for Arab landholders. One such change was the retroactive extension of the limitation period

> from ten to fifteen, or in some cases, twenty years. The Law of Limitation resulted in landholders, who had fulfilled all the requirements under Article 78 and had acquired property rights to the land, losing their rights due to the retroactive extension of the period.[5]

A person unable to prove that he continually possessed and cultivated the land for a period beginning before 1943 now had to prove that he had possessed and cultivated the land for a period of at least twenty years, that is, until at least 1963. "It has been estimated that the extension of the limitation period by the Law of Limitation resulted in the expropriation of more than 200,000 dunams of land from Arab possession."[6]

ISRAEL ACCUSED OF REINTERPRETED ARTICLE 43 OF THE HAGUE REGULATIONS OF 1907

Ronit Levine-Schnur explains that Israel exhibited a dual approach regarding the territories.[7] On the one hand, it complied with the norms of belligerent occupation. This included the provision of Article 43 in the Hague Regulations, 1907, concerning the occupier's duty "to restore, and ensure, as far as possible, public order and safety, while respecting, unless absolutely prevented, the laws in force in the country."[8] Accordingly, a military commander was in charge of the area and a Civil Administration was assembled in order to address non-military issues based on the laws that existed before the occupation. The acts of the Military Commander and the Civil Administration's Head are subject to review of the Israeli Supreme Court. On the other hand, Israel—and in particular certain influential interest groups within it—perceives the West Bank as part of the natural and promised homeland of the Jewish people. Under this approach, settling and residing in the Area is not only permitted but it is also a religious duty. Israel thus employed a policy of de-facto annexation of the land, not including the protected inhabitants. The principal way to do so was to reinterpret, among others, Article 43 of the Hague Regulations 1907.[9]

David Kretzmer explains in *al Naazer v. Commander of Judea and Samaria* that the petitioners' sought to challenge the state land system. The supplicants' claimed that under Jordanian law regular courts decided land claims. By investing "power over such claims in the hands of an appeals committee rather than the courts itself, the military governor had changed local law and thereby exceeded his authority under international law."[10]

Justice Meir Shamgar rejected this argument by pointing out the regulation 55 of The Hague Regulations which explains the occupying power "having a duty in safeguarding the capital of public property and administer them in accordance with the rules of usufruct."[11] He cited experts in the field of international law who state that when doubt arises whether property is public or private, the presumption shall be that property is public until ownership has been established. Due to the fact that military authorities are not subject to the jurisdiction of the local courts (which have general jurisdiction over land disputes), the appeals committee was authorized to deal with such disputes, thus giving residents remedy if they objected to certification of land as state land. Shamgar stated that by doing so local residents were given rights that they would not have had had the authorities relied exclusively on Article 43 of the Hague Regulations.

PRIVATE AND PUBLIC DISPUTES INTERTWINE?

David M. Philips writes, "Article 46 of the Hague Regulations bars an occupying power from confiscating private property. And it is on this point that the loudest cries against the settlements have been based. Israel did requisition land from private Arab owners to establish some early settlements, but requisitioning differs from confiscation (compensation is paid for use of the land), and the establishment of these settlements was based on military necessity."[12]

Ronit Schnur-Levin suggests that private and public disputes intertwine. In her paper she explains that as the number of disputes and complaints about private takeovers grew larger between Israelis and Palestinians, evidence for violent activities in relation to land conflicts began to pile up. "The Military Commander (MC) and the Civil Administration began to realize the potential for bloodshed over land possession."[13] Reacting to that, the MC took the decision of prioritizing the principles of rule of law and public order over what was until then conceived as beyond public power. Thus, the MC decided that even though the disputes concerned private property and private acts, they were not private disputes, but rather a matter of public order. The consequences that followed were a stricter interpretation to the substantive law. It suggested that if Palestinians ceased to cultivate their lands, the land may become—under some conditions—public land, but not an abandoned land that can be subject to adverse possession claims. Furthermore, the MC argued that in order to minimize incentives for land disputes, the laws of adverse possession should be read in line with equity demands and in accordance with modern-day needs. It was argued that "In the modern world, a time of diminishing resources, there is no justification for encouraging individuals to seize lands. Land distribution should be achieved through public mechanisms that are just and equal. "[14]

Appropriation of land without governmental approval is understood as morally wrong and a basis for anarchy, more so when taking into consideration the terms of belligerent occupation.

THE STANCE OF B'TSELEM

B'Tselems' report "Under the Guise of Legality: Israel's Declarations of State Land in the West Bank," began by giving a brief historical background in which they assert that "according to Israel the declaration policy [issuing declarations of state land] was based on the land laws applying in the West Bank in general, and on the Ottoman Land Code of 1858 in particular. Since the Code was in force at the time Israel occupied the West Bank, Israeli authorities claimed that they are required to respect it under international law, which stipulates that the occupying force may change existing legislation only if imperative military needs or the benefit of the local population necessitate such a change."[15] Israel admits that the fact that "the Ottoman land laws constitute the broad foundation of the land laws in Judea and Samaria" creates "an anachronistic situation that is almost without precedent."[16]

Martin Bunton writes, "one of the main objectives of the 1858 Ottoman Land Code was the economic and financial one of bringing as much *mahlul* and *mewat* land under cultivation as possible in the belief that the individual was better equipped to do so than the state. As soon as they were able, the British administration turned this around and, in order to free as large an area as possible to be vested in the state, the tendency emerged to define the indigenous rights as narrowly as possible."[17]

During the first twelve years of Israel's military occupation of the West Bank, the issue of state land was not controversial or a focus of dispute between the military government and the Palestinian population. At the time, Israeli authorities took a static approach toward state land, maintaining that state land was the land registered as government property by the countries that previously controlled the area—Britain and Jordan. Israel considered land that had not been registered as state land prior to 1967 to be privately owned by Palestinians, or, at least, land whose ownership had not been clarified (in which case it could not be deemed government property). Accordingly, for the first twelve years of the Israeli occupation, no declarations of state land were made. In the period from 1967 to 1979, the principal mechanism that Israel used to take control of land for the purpose of building settlements was by issuing requisition orders for military needs. During this period, Israel requisitioned 31,000 dunams, primarily for the building of settlements. When the land was requisitioned, the military government forced the landowners to "lease" it to the state and offered to pay for its use.

In the 1970s, Israeli governments claimed that the settlements served a clear military need and that the authorities could therefore requisition privately-owned land belonging to residents of the occupied territory for that reason. In three cases, the Israeli Supreme Court sitting as the High Court of Justice (HCJ) accepted this claim, holding that "taking possession of private property in occupied territory to build a civilian settlement does not contravene the principles of international customary law that an Israeli court considers, if establishment of the settlement is required for military needs of the authorities occupying the territory."[18]

International law allows an occupying country to temporarily requisition private land in an occupied territory, provided it does so to meet imperative military needs.[19]

This practice came to an end in 1979, with the HCJ's ruling in the Elon Moreh case. In its ruling, the court held that, in the specific case of Elon Moreh, the requisition of land was intended not to meet military needs but for settlement purposes, and therefore contravened international law.[20] However, the HCJ did not forbid in principle requisition of private Palestinian land for the purpose of settlement. The court held that so long as the military or security consideration is dominant in the decision to issue the requisition order, the military commander may requisition private land to build settlements. But if the dominant objective is to build a civilian settlement, and the security objectives are secondary, if they exist, the military commander is not entitled to requisition the land.

B'Tselem accuses Israel, "in the context of the declaration policy," of "applying a much stricter criterion than that of the cultivation doctrine that was set by the Mandatory courts and applied in in the West Bank under Jordanian rule as well."[21] And,

> According to the Israeli interpretation, in the case of a parcel that is mostly rocky and the cultivated area is located in a distinct part, the cultivated area must be distinguished from the rest of the parcel. In such a case, the rocky part of the parcel will be declared state land, while the cultivated area will be defined as private property. In the common case where it is not possible to distinguish between the cultivated parts and the rocky land, the farmer must prove that he cultivated at least 50 percent of the total area of the parcel. If the combined area of all the cultivated patches is under 50 percent, the entire parcel is declared state land, leaving the farmer with no rights to it whatsoever.
>
> In applying this requirement to the West Bank, Israel relied on rulings of Israeli courts in the 1960s.[22]

The "50 percent rule" is an Israeli judicial doctrine that has played a pivotal role in deciding disputes between the Israeli government and Palestinian landholders under Article 78 of the Ottoman Land Law. The judicial doctrine was used by Haifa district judges and military appeal boards to determine whether private claimants of land in rocky and hilly patches cultivated areas had fulfilled requirement of Article 78. The rule was a change from the British Mandate doctrine of "reasonable cultivation," which considered the nature of the land in question and required only "such regular cultivation as is reasonable possible, having regard to the nature of the land and the crops for which it is suitable."[23] The 50 percent rule made it tougher for private landholders to acquire rights by requiring them to prove cultivation of at least 50 percent of a parcel's surface area, regardless of its nature or the portion of its surface area that was covered by large stones. The rule itself, which became a binding, Israeli judicial doctrine evolved in the central Galilee region and was shaped by the local land disputes by the state and by Palestinian citizens of Israel living in the region. The region had not yet undergone settlement of title, or "land settlement" (the system of survey, mapping, and land registration initiated by the Mandate government and adopted by Israel in 1948). According to the terms of the system, this meant that the land registries were incomplete and that the state's recognition of ownership rights in the region had not yet been finalized. In response to the growing number of disputes reaching the Supreme Court, justices established rules to interpret and reinterpret certain Ottoman Land Laws relevant to the disputes.

In their rulings, the District Courts accepted the State Attorney's Office's interpretation of Article 78 of the Land Code, whereby in the case of cultivation of scattered patches of land, the claimant for ownership of the parcel must prove that he cultivated a substantial portion of its area.

The 50 percent rule is one of the doctrines which has worked to the advantage of the state and to the disadvantage of Palestinian claimants.[24]

In April 1961, Justice Haim Cohn, in his ruling, abandoned the Mandate doctrine of "reasonable cultivation" by ruling that since only 20 percent of a parcel was cultivated in 1945, the cultivation criterion had not been met. Eight months later, Chief Justice Yitzhak Olshan "continued this praxis by beginning to formulate a cultivation criterion based on the ratio of cultivated land to uncultivated land."[25] According to the evolving rule, fully cultivated portions of otherwise uncultivated parcels were to be severed off and awarded to the cultivators, while the uncultivated portions were to be awarded to the state. In a ruling in April 1962, Justice Cohn stipulated that Article 78 required that most of the parcel be cultivated. And in June 1962, Justice Olshan remanded a decision to the High District Court for reconsideration in accordance with the 50 percent rule. Within a few months the new doctrine had evolved to require proof of cultivation of at least 50 percent of a parcel in order to acquire land rights by virtue of Article 78. Israeli officials did not present their land claims as imported Israeli law or a change in local law. They rather anchored them in the dictates of already existing military legislation and international law (the right of the occupying power to secure state land in place of the ousted sovereign). As Jordanian land law had "the same statutory basis as Israeli land law in the 1950s and 1960s others could employ the same land–claiming methods in the West Bank as in the Galilee and present them as being within the letter of the law."[26] Israeli Supreme Court's approach in the early 1960s presented the 50 percent rule as "a clarifying test necessary for assessing whether a parcel had been reasonably cultivated and not as a fundamental change in local law."[27]

Jordanian law had no 50 percent rule and no other recently generated Article 78 case law. The reason for this might be due to the limited lawmaking role of courts in Jordan's continental legal system, in contrast to the centrality of court-made law in Israel's common law system. It also stemmed from the limited nature of Jordanian state land claims during the Jordanian rule, which resulted in relatively few disputes between the state and private claimants.

Israel military legislation formalized the practice of making declarations on land that was once cultivated for the prescriptive period, but where cultivation ceased at some subsequent point.

An assistant to the legal advisor for Judea and Samaria (West Bank), explained the objective of the change: A person who worked the land for ten or more years, and then abandoned it completely without have first registered it in his name—ostensibly has no right in the land.

The practice is to regard the rights of a person who cultivated *Miri* land for a sufficient period as expired if he abandoned and discontinued cultivation of the land for at least ten years . . . Therefore, if he ceased cultivating the land for at least ten years, it is regarded as having become the state's property by prescriptive right.

The practice regarding unregistered *Miri* land whose cultivation ceased is very important nowadays. Judea and Samaria contain large sections of hilly areas that were cultivated by terrace farming. . . . A gradual process of abandonment of terrace land began in Palestine, and already by the nineteenth century, many terraces had been dismantled.

Israel contends that although the declaration policy was not adopted by the states that ruled the West Bank before 1967, in practice, its results were not different from the outcome of land settlements undertaken by the British and Jordanian authorities. Registrations undertaken following land settlement procedures show that cultivated *Miri* land was registered in the name of the farmers, while uncultivated land was registered in the name of the state.

Plia Albeck, who headed the civilian department in the State Attorney's Office and was a primary driving force behind the declaration policy, concluded that "about 40 percent of Judea and Samaria land is state land, and this fact is reflected also in registrations of land that underwent land settlement, English or Jordanian. . . . Of course, the 40-percent figure is not a scientifically precise number, but rather a rough general estimate based on the registered and unregistered details. But it is true with respect both to areas that underwent land settlement and those that did not."[28]

In its ending remarks B'Tselem differ from the state's interpretation of the Ottoman Land Laws in three specifics.

1. Article 78 of the Ottoman Land Code in which The Mandate authorities and the Jordanian government considered patch cultivation of rocky land to meet the requirements of article 78 of the Ottoman Land Code. Both concluded that such patch cultivation grants the farmer ownership of the entire parcel. In contrast, Israel applied in the West Bank a strict

reading of article 78. According to its interpretation, in rocky areas, only cultivation encompassing at least 50 percent of the total area of the parcel will grant ownership rights to the farmer. By changing the interpretation of article 78 of the Land Code, which had been customary in the West Bank before 1967, Israel justified its decision to declare large areas of rocky mountain land that were under patch cultivation as government property, despite the position of the states who ruled the West Bank prior to 1967, who considered these lands to be private Palestinian property.

2. Israel also disregarded the judgments of the Mandatory Supreme Court and of Israel's Supreme Court, whereby a person who cultivated unregistered *Miri* land for ten years acquired ownership rights in the land, so that cessation of cultivation afterwards does not prejudice his rights, even if the land was not registered on his name in the land registry. By amending the law, within the framework of a change to the Order Concerning Government Property, Israel created a legal situation in which cessation of cultivation for several years completely nullified the person's rights in the land, even if he or his family had cultivated it for decades before.
3. Classification of designated *Matruka* land as government property. With respect to designated *Matruka* land—primarily grazing land used by residents of a specific village for many years—Israeli declaration policy deviated from the way the states that previously ruled the West Bank had applied the law and disregarded the binding court judgments. Unlike the situation with *Miri* land to which private persons can acquire rights, designated *Matruka* is by definition public land assigned for the specific use of members of a particular community and is not government property.[29]

THE STANCE OF PEACE NOW

Peace Now accuses Israel of coming up with “legal acrobatics” by “declaring” instead of “confiscating” land. By doing so, Peace Now refer to the Israeli polices as a “draconian interpretation”[30] of the Ottoman Land Law. As mentioned, land that is not cultivated for several years in a row becomes the property of the empire (predated modern states). This law was created with the aim of encouraging maximal land usage and enlarging the empire’s income through taxation. Through this interpretation of the Ottoman law, Israel has succeeded in taking over 900,000 dunams, or 16% of the West Bank. Declaration of state land is only possible if the land is not officially registered in the land registry as property of a specific individual.

An alternative record of ownership exists in local taxation books. Since Ottoman times, the authorities collected property tax in accordance with listed ownerships, even if land was not necessarily recorded in the land registry. This listing is much less thorough or exact. According to Israeli military law, the tax book is not a sufficient proof of ownership. In order to buy or sell land, for instance, the land must be officially registered or be in the process of being registered.

Peace Now claims that Israel, on the one hand, has stopped the process of land registration. On the other hand, it has treated all unregistered lands as not privately owned, even if it was recorded as private in the tax books, unless it was cultivated.

The result is that land which Palestinians see as privately owned and is recorded in the village tax books, could be seen by Israel as public land or state land, as long as it is not cultivated. This is why Israel claims that the declaration of state land does not change the status of the land but only affirms it, and therefore should not be considered as confiscation.

THE STANCE OF THE EDMUND LEVY REPORT

The Edmund Levy report was submitted to the Israeli government on June 21, 2012. It was written by Edmund Levy, retired Supreme Court Justice, Tehiya Shapira, retired District Court Judge member, and former ambassador Alan Baker. The Levy Report begin quoting a verdict from High Court of Justice. "As a rule, illegal construction situated on private land will be removed, and at the same time, the appropriate professional levels have been instructed to act towards regulating the planning status of structures located on state land; in places where such regulation will be decided upon, all this in accordance with the additional relevant considerations that apply to each and every area."[31] In HCJ 9060/08, *Dar Yassin et al. v. the Minister of Def et al.*, petitions were filed with the High Court against the illegal construction of structures on a site next to the Beit El settlement. Following a series of hearings the State notified the court of its adoption of a policy concerning the demolition of illegal building on private land and the arrangement of construction on State land. As a result of this policy, illegal construction located on private land would be removed. The Court gave a judgment giving effect to the State's undertaking to ensure the removal of the illegal structures within one year of the filing of said notification. The Levy Report was written pursuant to the above quotation and was asked, among other things, to provide recommendations towards: (a) where it would be possible to legalize or remove construction, (b) ensuring the existence of a proper procedure to clarify matters related to real estate issues in the area, in accordance with the principles of justice and fairness of the Israeli judicial and administrative system, in consideration of the laws that apply in the area, including whether there is a need for changes to ensure transparency, equality, the removal of obstructions and the streamlining of processes and procedures to the extent these are required.[32]

The authors of the Levy Report emphasized that they refrained from take any position as to the political wisdom of settlement activity as a whole but will rather acted in their "capacity as legal experts whose duty it is to rule solely according to the law."[33]

The Report takes up several representatives that attest that issue of settlements is a simple one inasmuch as it is prohibited according to international law. That is the view of Peace Now, B'Tselem, Yesh Din and the Association for Civil Rights in Israel (ACRI). "The approach taken by these organizations is a reflection of the position taken by the Palestinian leadership and some in the international community, who view Israel's status as that of a 'military occupier,' and the settlement endeavor as an entirely illegal phenomenon. This approach denies any Israeli or Jewish right to these territories."[34] Consequently, according to this approach, the provisions of international law regarding the matter of occupation apply to Israel as a military occupier (i.e., ICRC, "Regulations concerning the Laws and Customs of War on Land," The Hague, October 18, 1907), which govern the relationship between the occupier the occupied territory, and the Fourth Geneva Convention "Relative to the Protection of Civilian Persons in Time of War," Geneva, August 12, 1949.[35] According to these regulations, it is forbidden in principle to seize personal property, although the occupying power has the right to enjoy all the advantages derivable from the use of the property of the occupied state, and public property that is not privately owned without changing its fixed nature.

In this context, the authors of the Levy Report

> were presented with an approach by some of the abovementioned organizations, whereby they do not accept the premise that the lands that do not constitute personal property are state lands. It was claimed that in the absence of orderly registration of most of the land in Judea and Samaria, and precise registration of the rights of the local inhabitants, it is reasonable to assume that the local population is entitled to benefit from land that is neither defined nor registered as privately-owned land. From this it follows that the use of land for the purpose of the establishment of Israeli settlements impinges on the rights of the

> local population, which is a protected population according to the Convention, and Israel, as an occupying power, is obliged to safeguard these rights and not deny them by exploiting the land for the benefit of its own population.[36]

The Levy Report was also presented with a different approach by the Regavim movement and by the Benjamin Regional Council.

> They are of the view that Israel is not an "Occupying Power" as determined by international law inter alia because the territories of Judea and Samaria were never a legitimate part of any Arab state, including the kingdom of Jordan. Consequently, those conventions dealing with the administration of occupied territory and occupied populations are not applicable to Israel's presence in Judea and Samaria.
>
> According to this approach, even if the Geneva Convention applied, Article 49 was never intended to apply to the circumstances of Israel's settlements. Article 49 was drafted by the Allies after World War II to prevent the forcible transfer of an occupied population, as was carried out by Nazi Germany, which forcibly transferred people from Germany to Poland, Hungary and Czechoslovakia with the aim of changing the demographic and cultural makeup of the population. These circumstances do not exist in the case of Israel's settlement. Other than the fundamental commitment that applies universally by virtue of international humanitarian norms to respect individual personal property rights and uphold the law that applied in the territory prior to the IDF entering it, there is no fundamental restriction to Israel's right to utilize the land and allow its citizens to settle there, as long as the property rights of the local inhabitants are not harmed and as long as no decision to the contrary is made by the government of Israel in the context of regional peace negotiations.[37]

The Levy Report asks whether Israel's status is that of a military occupier with all this implies in accordance with international law? The authors do not think so, given the observation that

> the most reasonable interpretation of those provisions of international law appears to be that the accepted term "occupier" with its attending obligations, is intended to apply to brief periods of the occupation of the territory of a sovereign state pending termination of the conflict between the parties and the return of the territory or any other agreed upon arrangement. However, Israel's presence in Judea and Samaria is fundamentally different: Its control of the territory spans decades and no one can foresee when or if it will end; the territory was captured from a state (the kingdom of Jordan), whose sovereignty over the territory had never been legally and definitively affirmed, and has since renounced its claim of sovereignty; the State of Israel has a claim to sovereign right over the territory.[38]

The Levy Report states clearly:

> We are not convinced that an analogy may be drawn between this legal provision and those who sought to settle in Judea and Samaria, who were neither forcibly "deported" nor "transferred," but who rather chose to live there based on their ideology of settling the Land of Israel.
>
> We have not lost sight of the views of those who believe that the Fourth Geneva Convention should be interpreted so as also to prohibit the occupying state from encouraging or supporting the transfer of parts of its population to the occupied territory, even if it did not initiate it. However, even if this interpretation is correct, we would not alter our conclusions that Article 49 of the Fourth Geneva Convention does not apply to Jewish settlement in Judea and Samaria in view of the status of the territory according to international law.[39]

The Levy Report quotes the words of Lord James Balfour who, on November 2, published the declaration of which "Britain acknowledged the right of the Jewish people in the Land of Israel and expressed its willingness to promote a process that would ultimately lead to the establishment of a national home for it in this part of the world. This declaration reappeared in a different form, in the resolution of the Peace Conference in San Remo, Italy, which laid the foundations for the British Mandate over the Land of Israel and recognized the historical bond between the Jewish people and Palestine."[40]

"It should be noted here that the mandatory instrument (like the Balfour Declaration) noted only that "the civil and religious rights" of the inhabitants of Palestine should be protected, and no mention was made of the realization of the national rights of the Arab nation."[41]

"In August 1922 the League of Nations approved the mandate given to Britain, thereby recognizing, as a norm enshrined in international law, the right of the Jewish people to determine its home in the Land of Israel, its historic homeland, and establish its state therein." [42]

To complete the picture, the Levy Report add that "upon the establishment of the United Nations in 1945, Article 80 of its Charter determined the principle of recognition of the continued validity of existing rights of states and nations acquired pursuant to various mandates, including of course the right of the Jews to settle in the Land of Israel, as specified in the abovementioned documents"[43] : "Except as may be agreed upon in individual trusteeship agreements . . . nothing in this Chapter shall be construed in or of itself to alter in any manner the rights whatsoever of any states or any peoples or the terms of existing international instruments to which Members of the United Nations may respectively be parties."[44] In April 1950, Jordan annexed the territories of Judea and Samaria (West Bank), unlike Egypt, which did not demand sovereignty over the Gaza Strip. However, Jordan's annexation did not attain legal standing and was opposed even by the majority of Arab countries, until in 1988, Jordan declared that it no longer considered itself as having any status over that area. The Levy Report's belief is that by doing so, "this restored the legal status of the territory to its original status, i.e. territory designated to serve as the national home of the

Jewish people, which retained its 'right of possession' during the period of the Jordanian control, but was absent from the area for a number of years due to the war that was forced on it, but has since returned."[45]

"Most land disputes in Judea and Samaria are the result of the fact that there is no orderly and accessible registration of rights in real estate assets. Moreover, the public is not allowed to see some of the existing registry documents."[46] It is a significant obstacle that the "Civil Administration has not completed the land-survey process ('*seker*') that begun during the period of the Jordanian rule."[47]

In promoting stability and preventing uncertainty, the authors of the Levy Report believe that the residents of Judea and Samaria, Palestinians and Israelis alike, should be encouraged to register their rights in the land within a fixed period of time (four or five years seems a reasonable period), at the end of which time, anyone who has not carried out the registration will lose whatever rights he may have had. The report further suggests:

- In the event of conflicting claimants to land, it would be appropriate to adopt a policy whereby prior to any determination by the state regarding petitions for eviction or demolition, a thorough examination of the conflicting claims be conducted by a judicial tribunal dealing with land issues. This is all the more necessary with respect to claims of prior purchase or obsolescence, or where the possessor acted in good faith. Pending such determination, state authorities should be instructed to refrain from taking any position in land conflicts and taking irreversible measures, such as eviction or demolition of buildings on the property.
- To this end and with a view to facilitating accessibility by local residents to judicial tribunals, the authors suggest the establishment of courts for the adjudication of land disputes in Judea and Samaria, or alternatively, extending the jurisdiction of district

> court judges in order to enable them to handle land disputes in Judea and Samaria in their courts.[48]

The Levy Report also emphatically states that "the point of departure for the report's position is, as noted, that Jews have the legal right to settle in all of Judea and Samaria, and at the very least, in those areas under the control of Israel by virtue of agreements with the Palestinian Authority."[49]

The determination of the Levy Report that the territories are not occupied caused a "sensation." According to Professor Aeyal Gross, who teaches at the Faculty of Law at Tel Aviv University, the Levy Report reliance on the Balfour Declaration suggests that the Committee adopted the "colonial perspective that had granted Britain the authority to determine the future of the territory while disregarding the currently widespread recognition of peoples' right to self—determination. Its conclusions ignored the presence of an occupied Palestinian population living in these areas and the denial of its rights."[50] Prior to the Levy Report, Israel had not categorically denied its status as occupier and had agreed to endorse a different aspect of an occupier's legal obligations, as laid out in The Hague Regulations. The Levy Committee, however, seemed to take this policy a step further when claiming that these areas are not occupied territory at all in order to reject the argument calling for application of the Geneva Convention. In so doing, Gross argues that the Committee entirely disregarded the implications of such a declaration for the legality of the Israeli army exercising its authority in the territories, which do rely on the Hague Regulations. In hundreds of its judgements, the High Court of Justice has addressed the territories as one under belligerent occupation. For example, the Court accepted the state's position that the army is permitted to seize lands for military purposes based on the authority of the military commander in an area under belligerent occupation, as stated in the Hague Regulations.

The government chose not to adopt the Levy Report formally because doing so would put Israel at odds with international community, which regards the West Bank as an occupied territory, though in its policies on the unauthorized outposts it endorsed the Report's spirit.[51]

NOTES

1. .DF Mag Corps, Issues of real estate, construction and municipal law http://www.law.idf.il/602-2385-en/Patzar.aspx

2. B'Tselem, "Under the Guise of Legality: Israel's Declarations of State Land in the West Bank," report, February 2012, 33, https://www.btselem.org/download/201203_under_the_guise_of_legality_eng.pdf (accessed May 25, 2018).

3. Ronit Schnur-Levine. "Private Property and Public: Power In the Occupied West Bank," *European Property Law Journal* 6, no. 2 (August 2017): 124

4. See *The Ottoman Land Code*, trans. Frank Ongley (London: Forgotten Books, 2015), 41.

5. Alexandre (Sandy) Kedar, "The Legal Transformation of Ethnic Geography: Israeli Law and the Palestinian Landholder, 1948–1967," *New York University Journal of International Law and Politics* 33, no. 4 (Summer 2001): 971.

6. Kedar, "Legal Transformation of Ethnic Geograph," 973.

7. Ronit Schnur-Levine. "Private Property and Public: Power In the Occupied West Bank," *European Property Law Journal* 6, no. 2 (August 2017): 122–41.

8. International Committee of the Red Cross (ICRC), "Convention (IV) Respecting the Laws and Customs of War on Land and Its Annex: Regulations Concerning the Laws and Customs of War on Land, Annex to the Convention: Article 43. Section 3. Military Authority Over the Territory of the Hostile State," The Hague, October 18, 1907, https://ihl-databases.icrc.org/ihl/WebART/195-200053? (accessed May 25, 2018).

9. Schnur-Levine, "Private Property and Public," 124.

10. David Kretzmer, *The Occupation of Justice: The Supreme Court of Israel and the Occupied Territories* (Albany: State University of New York Press, 2002), 91.

11. David Kretzmer, *The Occupation of Justice: The Supreme Court of Israel and the Occupied Territories* (Albany: State University of New York Press, 2002), 91.

12. David M. Philips, "The Illegal Settlements Myth," *Commentary*, December 1, 2009, https://www.commentarymagazine.com/articles/the-illegal-settlements-myth/ (accessed May 26, 2018).

13. Schnur-Levine, "Private Property and Public," 132.

14. Schnur-Levine, "Private Property and Public," 132.

15. B'Tselem, "Under the Guise of Legality," 6.

16. B'Tselem, "Under the Guise of Legality," 6.

17. Martin Bunton, "Demarcating the British Colonial State: Land Settlement in the Palestine *Jiftlik* Villages of Sajad and Qazaza," in *New Perspectives on Property and Land in the Middle East*, ed. Roger Owen (Cambridge, MA: Center for Middle Eastern Studies, Harvard University Press, 2000), 128.

18. B'Tselem, "Under the Guise of Legality," 9.

19. See, for example, Article 52 of the International Committee of the Red Cross (ICRC), "Convention (IV) Respecting the Laws and Customs of War on Land and Its Annex: Regulations Concerning the Laws and Customs of War on Land. Annex to the Convention," The Hague, October 18, 1907, https://ihl-databases.icrc.org/ihl/WebART/195-200053? (accessed May 25, 2018).

20. Israel, High Court of Justice, *Duweikat et al. v. Government of Israel et al.* Judgment. HCJ 390/79. October 22, 1979. http://www.hamoked.org/files/2010/1670_eng.pdf (accessed June 7, 2018).

21. B'Tselem, "Under the Guise of Legality," 37.

22. B'Tselem, "Under the Guise of Legality," 37–38.

23. Geremy Forman, "A Tale of Two Regions: Diffusion of the Israeli '50 Percent Rule' from the Galilee to the Occupied West Bank," *Law & Social Inquiry* 34, no 3 (Summer 2009): 673.

24. Geremy Forman, "A Tale of Two Regions," 680.

25. Geremy Forman, "A Tale of Two Regions," 680.

26. Geremy Forman, "A Tale of Two Regions," 686.

27. Geremy Forman, "A Tale of Two Regions," 687.

28. "Under the Guise of Legality," 47. For further reading see also, David Kretzmer, *The Occupation of Justice: The Supreme Court of Israel and the Occupied Territories* (Albany: State University of New York Press, 2002), 90.

29. B'Tselem, "Under the Guise of Legality," 59. In the verdict Israel, *Al-Uqbi et al. v. State of Israel*, Case [C.A.] 4220/12, Supreme Court Judgement of May 14, 2015, there is a reasoning on grazing rights. It is explained that the Ottoman Land Code distinguishes between grazing lands that were assigned to a specific public and grazing lands that are within the boundaries of the village and which serve its residents, even without having been assigned thereto. Section 97 of the Land Code entitles the residents of the village to an exclusive right to graze their herds in areas that were assigned to them and to prevent strangers from doing so. By contrast, under Section 105 the residents of the village are only entitled to a right to graze in the areas that are adjacent to their village without paying taxes therefor, but it does not allow them to prevent strangers from grazing in these areas. Furthermore, while the grazing rights under Section 97 are protected against both private individuals and against the State, grazing rights under Section 105 do not prevent the State from expropriating the land or granting it to any person as *Miri* land.

30. Peace Now, "Methods of Confiscation—How Does Israel Justify and Legalize Confiscation of Lands? *Peace Now*, January 1, 2009, http://peacen-

ow.org.il/en/methods-of-confiscation-how-does-israel-justify-and-legalize-confiscation-of-lands?lang=en (accessed May 26, 2018). Peace Now, What is a declaration of state land? September 9, 2014,http://peacenow.org.il/en/what-is-a-declaration-of-state-land(accessed June 7, 2018).Israel does not deviate from the British policies, as shown by Roger Owen and Barbara J Smith who attest that the British policies sought to prevent the cultivation of state lands without the Administration´s permission (see *New Perspectives on Property and Land in the Middle East*, ed. Roger Owen, 28–32; and Smith, *The Roots of Separatism in Palestine: British Economic Policy, 1920-1929* [Syracuse, NY: Syracuse University Press, 1993], 98).

31. Israel, "The Levy Commission Report on the Legal Status of Building in Judea and Samaria," trans. Regavim (2014), June 21, 2012, 4, http://www.regavim.org/levy-report-translated-into-english/ (accessed May 26, 2018).

32. Israel, "Levy Commission Report, " 4.

33. Israel, "Levy Commission Report, " 4.

34. Israel, "Levy Commission Report, " 5.

35. International Committee of the Red Cross (ICRC). "Convention (IV) Relative to the Protection of Civilian Persons in Time of War." Article 49. Geneva. August 12, 1949. https://ihl-databases.icrc.org/ihl/WebART/380-600056 (accessed May 25, 2018).

36. Israel, "Levy Commission Report, " 6-7.

37. Israel, "Levy Commission Report, " 7.

38. Israel, "Levy Commission Report, " 8.

39. Israel, "Levy Commission Report, " 9.

40. Israel, "Levy Commission Report, " 10.

41. Israel, "Levy Commission Report, " 10.

42. Israel, "Levy Commission Report, " 11.

43. Israel, "Levy Commission Report, " 11.

44. United Nations, *Charter of the United Nations*, June 26, 1945, http://www.un.org/en/charter-united-nations/index.html (accessed May 25, 2018); see Article 80, Paragraph 1, http://www.un.org/en/sections/un-charter/chapter-xii/ (accessed may 31, 2018).

45. Israel, "Levy Commission Report," 12.

46. Israel, "Levy Commission Report," 61.

47. Israel, "Levy Commission Report," 61.

48. Israel, "Levy Commission Report," 76.

49. Israel, "Levy Commission Report," 62.

50. Aeyal M. Gross, *The Writing On the Wall: Rethinking the International Law of Occupation* (Cambridge: Cambridge University Press, 2017), 159.

51. Gross, *The Writing On the Wall*, 160.

Chapter Three

Article 43 of The Hague Regulations

The International Committee of the Red Cross (ICRC) in its "Convention (IV) Respecting the Laws and Customs of War on Land and Its Annex: Regulations Concerning the Laws and Customs of War on Land. Annex to the Convention: Article 43," states: "The authority of the legitimate power having in fact passed into the hands of the occupant, the latter shall take all the measures in his power to restore, and ensure, as far as possible, public order and safety, while respecting, unless absolutely prevented, the laws in force in the country."[1]

Gerald M. Adler of the *Journal* notes that, "the substantive land laws applying in the West Bank are based principally on the 1858 Ottoman Land Code, amended by the British Mandate and Jordanian Governments under their respective jurisdictions. They remain substantially unaltered.[2] Further he writes: "The land law had two main objectives: (i) to bring vacant and uncultivated land into productive use in order to accommodate population growth and create employment; and (ii) to strengthen the Government's tax base." and that "the law provided only for registration of land transactions, which are personal in nature and no guarantee of good title." [3]

Jeremy Bob Yonah writes in his article for the *Jerusalem Post*, that "though it is not widely known, the legal status of the West Bank was decided by 1963." Back then,

> [Israel Defence Forces] IDF military advocate-general (MAG) Meir Shamgar had already authored a treatise about what to do regarding legal issues if Israel took control of the West Bank.[4]
>
> Shamgar's ideas, embodied by a series of IDF military orders issued soon after the IDF took over the West Bank, have dominated the Israeli debate for the 50 years since then. The starting point for the discussion was Shamgar and Israel's acceptance of the 1907 Hague Regulations applying to the West Bank. This means Israeli control over the West Bank falls into the category of "belligerent occupation." In less fancy language, it means that Israel has not annexed the land and is holding it temporarily. Further, it means that Israel has certain obligations not to change the face of the land or harm the rights of the local people already there—the Palestinians.[5]

According to Eyal Benvenisti, *The International Law of Occupation*, "The Hague Regulations assumed that upon gaining control, the occupant would establish its authority over the occupied area. . . . In 1907 there was no need to emphasize this point: the establishment of a system of administration by the occupant was widely accepted in practice. Today, however such practice is the rare exception rather than the rule."[6]

In a publication by Centre on Housing Rights and Evictions (CHOHRE), and BADIL Resource Center for Palestinian Residency and Refugees Rights, "Ruling Palestine," writes that when the Israeli Defence Forces (IDF) entered the Territories in 1967, the military commanders published proclamations that the prevailing law would remain in force, subject to changes made by military order or proclamation. The first of this kind came on June 6, 1967, when the Regional Commander of the Israeli Defence Forces issued the *Proclamation on Law and Administration (Proclamation*

No. 2) which, "stipulated that laws already in existence would remain in force, as long as they did not conflict with any other Israeli regulations. In the event that they did, Israeli law would supersede any pre-existing law."[7]

CHOHRE and BADIL's report goes on to say: "As of 1992, ninety-six of the full set of Military Orders operating in the West Bank had been issued specifically as 'amendments' to Jordanian law. Israel maintains that such amendments are essential to its rule in the West Bank."[8]

David M. Philips's article notes, "Israel has for the most part continued to follow Jordanian law in the West Bank, despite its position that Jordan itself had illegally occupied it. Israel's stance has been criticized as contradictory, but general continuance of Jordanian law can be justified on grounds of legal stability and long-term reliance reflected in most legal systems, including international law."[9]

In Yonah's article it is explained by Hebrew University Law School dean and Israel Democracy Institute Fellow Yuval Shany that, "agreeing to apply the Hague principles 'was the only possible decision since there was no political decision to annex the West Bank' . . . Israel could have decided to extend Israeli law to the West Bank, as was done in east Jerusalem, 'but the government did not want to make that political decision,' so accepting the international law obligations and limits of the Hague Regulations was left as 'the only option.'"[10] As attested by Shany, "there has always been a debate about the application of the Geneva Conventions to the West Bank."[11]

The question of why Israel accepted application of The Hague Regulations while argued that the Geneva Conventions do not apply [and that Israel only voluntarily applies the humanitarian provisions of the Geneva Conventions] has, according to Shany, to do with the fact that the Geneva conventions refer to "prior sovereign state. The Hague Regulations does not, it just talks about entering enemy/disputed territory."[12]

Benvenisti states that another important distinction between the Geneva Convention and The Hague Regulations is, while the former caters to the interests of individuals under foreign rule, the latter "primarily protect governmental interests."[13]

Israel took control of the West Bank from Jordan, but Jordan had, according to most countries in the world and the United Nations, illegally annexed the West Bank in a land grab during the 1948 war. There was no way that Israel would recognize Jordan as having been rightfully and legally in control of the West Bank, so the Israeli position was that when it took over the West Bank, it had taken over disputed territory as part of a war.

Accepting The Hague Regulations without accepting Geneva Conventions meant that Israel would protect Palestinian individual human rights, without recognizing Jordanian sovereign land rights. Israel could now stake its claims to the West Bank in negotiations under UN Security Council Resolution 242, which dictates the terms of peace negotiations between Israel and its Arab neighbours. "Despite Israel's nonrecognition of the Jordanian annexation of the West Bank, it respected the latter's existing laws in order to maintain public order."[14] During the entire period of occupation, the basic principle of retention of preoccupation law, subject to the occupant's power under The Hague Regulations to modify it from time to time, has been adhered to.

Shamgar set out this balance in a public speech in 1971 when he had moved on from being the MAG to becoming the attorney-general. It is assumed that Israel's position of accepting The Hague, but not Geneva, was designed by Shamgar to satisfy the political class's desire for flexibility on future issues of dividing territory.

Benvenisti refer to article 43 of the Hague Regulations as "The Framework of the Law of Occupation."[15] This concise article is the essence of the law of occupation. These words represent the culmination of prescriptive methods made throughout the nineteenth century by national courts, military manuals, and nonbinding international instruments. Article 43 is the cornerstone. Article 43 deals with the general powers of the occupant and as such, mentions the obligations and rights of the occupying power in the course of fulfilling its mission. Article 43 is a mini-constitution for the occupation administration. Obviously, from the Article itself "emerges the implicit recognition of the right of the occupant *not* to respect some of the local laws."[16]

PROLONGED OCCUPATION CREATES UNBRIDGEABLE CONFLICTS

Benvenisti explains that the phrases in Article 43, "public order" and what should be translated as "civil life" delimit the scope of the occupant's powers and duties.[17] In addition to that, the phrases itself are subjected to changing conception regarding the role of the central government in society. To nineteenth-century politicians and legal scholars, there was nothing problematic about recognizing the occupant's power to prescribe measures for the purpose of restoring and ensuring public order and civil life. Based on the then- prevailing notions of the proper role of central governments and assumptions as to the short duration and nature of war, giving this power to the occupant was quite undramatic on the part of the societies susceptible to occupations. At the time it was not expected that the occupant would have any self-interest in regulating social functions and duties. "Consequently, no one raised the possibility of the occupant's intervention in these areas to further its own policies" since one "viewed the likely motives of the occupant to be short-term military concerns, not infringe upon the local civil and criminal order."[18]

In the twentieth century, the "increasing regulation of the markets and other social activities by central governments, . . . the duty imposed on the occupant turned into a grant of authority to prescribe and create changes in a wide spectrum of affairs."[19] Article 43 was a convenient tool for the occupant: if it wished it could intervene in practically all aspects of life, if it was in its interest to refrain from action, it could invoke the limits imposed on its powers.

In *The Writing On the Wall*, Aeyal M. Gross notes that

> The balance between, on the one hand, humanitarian and human rights concerns pouring content into the notion of trust and, on the other, military necessities delimiting but never dismissing this trust, is thus the hallmark of the current law of occupation. The tensions inherent in such a situation are even more prominent in long-term occupations. The restriction on the occupant's authority to amend the laws of the country for the sake of reforms that might become necessary over the years underscores this point. In long-term occupations, the result may well be stagnation of all aspects of economic, political, cultural, and social existence, with harsh consequences for the population.[20]

The need to "restore" public order and civil life arises in the wake of the hostilities that disrupts them. The quest "to ensure" becomes more relevant as the occupation is protracted.

The requirement to "respect" the existing laws "unless absolutely prevented"[21] becomes meaningful when it is linked to the considerations that the occupants are entitled or required to weigh while contemplating the desirability of change in regard to the interest in stability and respect for the status quo. "Delineating the legitimate concerns of the occupant is however not enough. One must determine the proper balances: the desired balance between stability and change in general, and the balance"[22] between the conflicting considerations that the occupant faces in a particular matter. It appears "that the drafters of this phrase viewed military necessity as the sole relevant consideration that could "absolutely prevent" from maintain the old order."[23] Other scholars conceded other legitimate subjects for the occupant's lawmaking. Some are of the opinion "that the occupant might lawfully enact laws for nonmilitary goals."[24]

Further, Benvenisti notes that "the administration of the occupied territory is required to protect two sets of interests: first, to preserve the sovereign rights of the ousted government, and second, to protect the local population from exploitation of both their persons and their property by the occupant."[25] In a possible case of conflict, the occupant was supposed to prefer the interests of the government. It also had the duty to protect the local institutions against indigenous forces that might call for structural changes in the internal body politic.

From the exploration of Article 43 and its intellectual environment emerges a picture of the concept of occupations that prevailed at the turn of the century. The delegates to the Hague Peace Conferences conceived occupation as a transient situation, for the short period between hostilities and the imminent peace treaty, which would translate wartime victories into territorial concessions by the defeated party.

The occupant was expected to fulfill a positive role by filling the vacuum created by the ousting of the local government, and by maintaining its bases of power until the conditions for the latter's return were mutually agreed upon. The local population was similarly under a duty to abide by the occupant's exercise of authority. Benvenisti goes on to say,

> More and more issues gradually became the objects of unbridgeable conflicts of interests, as the occupant sought to intervene in the affairs of the territory under its control, and at the same time its acts had the potential of causing profound effects in both the public and the private sectors. It was no longer possible to expect the occupant to perform the function of the impartial trustee of the ousted sovereign or the local population; it was no longer feasible to demand that the occupant pay no heed to its own country's interests.[26]

RESPECT THE LAWS IN FORCE VERSUS FLEXIBILITY WHEN CONDITIONS CHANGE

According to David Kretzmer's *The Occupation of Justice*, "the principle of international law (articulated in Article 43) that an occupying power must respect the laws in force" in the occupied territory was formally recognized in 1967. When "capturing areas previously held by the enemy the military commanders issued proclamations that the prevailing law would remain in force, subject to such changes as would be made by military order."[27] He goes on to say, "the *term absolutely prevented* cannot be taken literally as some flexibility must be allowed in exercise of governmental functions in occupied territory, especially when the occupation is prolonged and conditions change."[28]

For example, in defense of trying to replace old laws with Israeli law in the West Bank, Justice Minister Ayelet Shaked said that "citizens living in the West Bank are being discriminated against under current Israeli law, which places them under military rule, unlike other citizens" and described "unregulated maternity leave for women employed in West Bank settlements and the lack of environmental laws as evidence of the bill's necessity. . . . What we're trying to do is to make the process more orderly. At the end of the day, hundreds of thousands of people live there, and just like you can't fire a woman for being pregnant in Israel, that should also apply to women in Judea and Samaria. Using this example, this law would apply in the same way to Palestinian women employed by Israeli businesses" beyond the Green Line, she said, "noting that civil law would not apply to Palestinians not employed by Israel."[29]

Shaked advanced a bill in February 2018 that aims at stripping the High Court of Justice of its jurisdiction to hear cases regarding West Bank land disputes. The proposal require Palestinians who claim ownership of land that has been built on by Israeli settlers to first petition the Jerusalem District Court. Jacob Magid article in the *Times of Israel* states that "according to a statement from Justice Minister Ayelet Shaked, who introduced the measure, the legislation seeks to accomplish three goals."[30] Magid also writes, "the first is to normalize the legal system in the West Bank, where the High Court rules on land disputes, entry permits, and Freedom of Information Law requests, as compared to Israelis living within the Green Line, who petition administrative courts on such matters."[31] In addition, the proposal will accomplish "that the burden of proof in High Court petitions is on the defendant rather than the plaintiff—a hierarchy that would be flipped in cases heard before a district court. . . . The legislation's third goal is explained by lighten the load of the High Court, which receives roughly 2,000 petitions a year."[32]

The Hague Regulations did not envision that a peace treaty between the rival parties would take such a long time to reach. In the nineteenth century, military defeats were soon followed by peace treaties and border modifications, and thus occupations were short lived.

Does the mere fact that the occupation lingers on, confer upon the occupant more powers than in a short-term occupation, or is it, rather the other way around? Below is the Israeli Supreme Court's take on this question. "Life does not stand still, and no administration, whether an occupation administration or another, can fulfill its duties with respect to the population if it refrains from legislating and from adapting the legal situation to the exigencies of modern times."[33]

In a prolonged occupation the maintenance of the status quo could prove insupportable to the local population. It would be wrong and even at times illegal, to freeze the legal situation and prevent adaptions when an occupation is extended.

The Supreme Court held that in light of the state belligerency, the occupying has not only the responsibility of ensuring order in the occupied territory, but also to deal with dangers presented from the occupied territory to the territory of the occupying power itself.

There could therefore be no real distinction between the narrow military needs of the occupying army and the wider security needs of the state. As a contrast, Benvenisti, expresses doubt whether the settlement policy is in line with Article 43 of the Hague Regulations, since it, in his view, "cannot be deemed as a matter of security of the occupation forces, and it is even more difficult to demonstrate its contribution to 'public order and civil life.'"[34] The Israeli Supreme Court states that with regard to the pure security aspect, there can be no doubted that the presence in the territories of settlements—even "civilian" settlements—of citizens of the occupying power contributes appreciably to security in that territory and makes it easier for the army to carry out its task. CHOHRE and BADIL in "Ruling Palestine," writes: "One does not have to be a military and security expert to realize that terrorist elements operate more easily in an area inhabited only by a population that is indifferent or is sympathetic towards the enemy than in an area where there are also persons likely to look out for them and to report any suspicious movement to the authorities."[35]

MORE POLITICS, LESS LAW

Much of what has happened with the settlements, since the legal status of the West Bank was decided 1963, had more to do with politics than with law. Until 1948, Judea and Samaria had always been an integral part of the Land of Israel (Eretz Israel). During the periods of the First and Second Temples, the Jews lived in the mountain area rather than in the coastal plain where most of modern Israel is located. Many Jewish symbols were linked to this area. Almost every place that was captured were the sites of graves of the forefathers of ancient Israel, and therefore they stirred recollections of biblical places about which every Israeli child had learned. Immediately after the Six Day War, Moshe Dayan declared that "We have returned to our people's holy places, to Shiloh and Anatot, and we will never leave them."[36] The war created an interaction between the feelings aroused by the war and the revival with the places which were the cradle of Jewish mythology.

In his book, *Zionism and Territory: The Socio-Territorial Dimensions of Zionist Politics*, Baruch Kimmerling makes some interesting remarks. The author gives an example of the Kiryat Arba/Hebron settlers. As a densely populated Arab center, the city of Hebron had been outside the initial Israeli "settlement map." On the other hand, Hebron is part of the mythological past: it is the location of the graves of some of the Jewish forefathers and until 1929 the site of an ancient Jewish community. The destruction of Hebron was a traumatic, central, event for the Jews in Palestine. Passover 1968. A religious group led by Moshe Levinger comes to Hebron with wishes to celebrate holiday there. The group rents a hotel near the center of the city and refuses to leave. They prolong their staying. Three months later the military agrees to ensure the group's safety on condition it will leave the hotel and move to a nearby area under military supervision. What happened was that the government had recognized the group in order to control it. The government was "forced to acknowledge the fact of a Jewish quarter near Kiryat Arba/Hebron."[37] According to Kimmerling, the Hebron group based its struggle on two principles of great potency in Israeli society:" personal fulfilment through pioneering and the return to a place perceived as belonging to the collectively in terms of both the recent past and Jewish mythology."[38]

First, the settlements ballooned from zero to a tiny smidgen of villages in the late 1960s. The 1973 election campaign focused on an attempt to intensify Israeli presence in the territories. The Minister of Defence proposed the certification of land purchases by both institutions and individuals (treating the territories as a frontier). This would legitimize what had been occurring since the end of 1972, when Jewish entrepreneurs, along with government and national institutions began to purchase considerable tracts of land, particularly in the West Bank.[39]

Events had taken an interesting turn. While in the past there was nothing more repugnant than the sale of land to Jews, and Israelis were forced to purchase land under the name of unknown companies in Lichtenstein, the ban had been lifted. Some Arabs were willing to sell land to Jews openly and the purchasers came with the seller to his Arab neighbours in order to receive a written certification from them stating the boundaries of the sold area.

Kimmerling observes that the defreezing of lands in the territories was almost identical to the process of the defreezing of Arab lands in the Mandatory Period. The flow of capital- both from national authorities, public institutions, private entrepreneurs and speculators—caused a sharp rise in land prices but also stimulated more and more Arabs to convert land to capital despite the community pressures against sales to Jews.

Baruch Kimmerling makes the assumption that the supply of lands for sale grew as Israeli control of the territories was seen as permanent both by landowners and purchases (who were prepared to invest more as the risk of loss declined and chance for profits increased).

After the 1973 War, the trend of sales and demands seems to have been reversed. This caused Moshe Dayan to be in favor of legalizing land purchases to achieve additional defreezing of land by encouraging investment by private individuals.[40] It seemed that with the Prime Minister Golda Meir support, Dayan's approach would be accepted by the majority. But Golda Meir changed her mind in the wake of the international uproar the proposal aroused. Meir also wanted to prevent a speculation by private entrepreneurs (Golda Meir was answering a question from Menachem Begin in the Israeli parliament regarding list of requests for land purchases-requests for acquisition of 50,000 dunams, 15,000, 5,000 and 2,000 when she realized that what was involved was land purchase for speculation).

Nevertheless, the matter was raised again in the election of 1974. In the matter of land purchase, primacy was granted to a national authority- the Israel Land Authority.

NOTES

1. International Committee of the Red Cross (ICRC),"Convention (IV) Respecting the Laws and Customs of War on Land and Its Annex: Regulations Concerning the Laws and Customs of War on Land. Annex to the Convention: Article 43. Section 3. Military Authority Over the Territory of the Hostile State," The Hague, October 18, 1907, https://ihl-databases.icrc.org/ihl/WebART/195-200053? (accessed May 25, 2018).
2. Gerald M. Adler, "West Bank: A Response," *Journal* (Scotland), September 14, 2009, http://www.journalonline.co.uk/Magazine/54-9/1006961.aspx (accessed May 24, 2018).
3. Adler, "West Bank: A Response."
4. Jeremy Bob Yonah, "50 Years Since 1967: What is the West Bank's Real Legal Status," *Jerusalem Post*, May 26, 2017, https://www.jpost.com/Magazine/50-years-of-law-versus-reality-493859 (accessed May 27, 2018).
5. Yonah, "50 Years Since 1967."
6. Eyal Benvenisti, *The International Law of Occupation*, new ed. (Princeton, NJ: Princeton University Press, 2004), 4–5.
7. Centre on Housing Rights and Evictions (CHOHRE), and BADIL Resource Center for Palestinian Residency and Refugees Rights, "Ruling Palestine: A History of the Legally Sanctioned Jewish-Israeli Seizure of Land and Housing in Palestine," May 2005, 79, http://www.badil.org/phocadownloadpap/Badil_docs/publications/Ruling%20Palestine.pdf (accessed May 25, 2018).
8. Centre on Housing Rights and Evictions (CHOHRE), and BADIL Resource Center for Palestinian Residency and Refugees Rights, "Ruling Palestine: A History of the Legally Sanctioned Jewish-Israeli Seizure of Land and Housing in Palestine," May 2005, 80, http://www.badil.org/phocadownloadpap/Badil_docs/publications/Ruling%20Palestine.pdf (accessed May 25, 2018).
9. David M. Philips, "The Illegal Settlements Myth," *Commentary*, December 1, 2009, https://www.commentarymagazine.com/articles/the-illegal-settlements-myth/ (accessed May 26, 2018).
10. Yuval Shany, quoted in Yonah, "50 Years Since 1967."
11. Yuval Shany, quoted in Yonah, "50 Years Since 1967."
12. Yuval Shany, quoted in Yonah, "50 Years Since 1967."
13. Benvenisti, *International Law of Occupation*, 110.
14. Benvenisti, *International Law of Occupation*, 114.

15. Benvenisti, *International Law of Occupation*, 7.
16. Benvenisti, *International Law of Occupation*, 9; emphasis in the original.
17. Benvenisti, *International Law of Occupation*, 9.
18. Benvenisti, *International Law of Occupation*, 10.
19. Benvenisti, *International Law of Occupation*, 10.
20. Aeyal M. Gross, *The Writing On the Wall: Rethinking the International Law of Occupation* (Cambridge: Cambridge University Press, 2017), 28–29.
21. Benvenisti, *International Law of Occupation*, 13.
22. Benvenisti, *International Law of Occupation*, 13.
23. Benvenisti, *International Law of Occupation*, 14.
24. Benvenisti, *International Law of Occupation*, 14.
25. Benvenisti, *International Law of Occupation*, 28.
26. Benvenisti, *International Law of Occupation*, 30.
27. David Kretzmer, *The Occupation of Justice: The Supreme Court of Israel and the Occupied Territories* (Albany: State University of New York Press, 2002), 61.
28. Kretzmer, *The Occupation of Justice*, 63; emphasis in the original.
29. Tamar Pileggi, "Shaked Revives Bid to Extend Civil Law to Settlements," *Times of Israel*, May 2, 2016, http://www.timesofisrael.com/shaked-to-revive-bill-to-extend-civil-law-to-settlements/ (accessed May 26, 2018).
30. Jacob Magid, "Bill Stripping High Court's Power to Adjudicate West Bank Land Disputes Advances," *Times of Israel*, February 25, 2018, https://www.timesofisrael.com/bill-seizing-high-courts-power-to-adjudicate-west-bank-land-disputes-advances/ (accessed May 31, 2018).
31. Magid, "Bill Stripping High Court's Power."
32. Magid, "Bill Stripping High Court's Power..
33. Israeli Supreme Court, quoted in Benvenisti, *International Law of Occupation*, 146.
34. Benvenisti, *International Law of Occupation*, 141. To compare with Benvenisti's view in *International Law of Occupation*, take a closer look at the state´s opinion that a military, security necessity and the establishment of a civilian community are not necessarily contradictory in Israel, High Court of Justice, *'Izzat Muhammad Mustafa Duweikat et 16 al. v. 1. Government of Israel 2. Minister of Defense 3. Military Commander for the Judea and Samaria Area 4. Nablus District Military Commander 5. Felix Menahem 6. Shvut Avraham*, Case HCJ 390/79, September 6-October 22, 1979, http://www.hamoked.org/files/2010/1670_eng.pdf (accessed May 25, 2018).
35. CHOHRE and BADIL, "Ruling Palestine."
36. Baruch Kimmerling, *Zionism and Territory: The Socio-Territorial Dimensions of Zionist Politics* (Berkeley: Institute of International Studies, University of California, 1983), 149.
37. Kimmerling, *Zionism and Territory*, 156.
38. Kimmerling, *Zionism and Territory*, 156.
39. Kimmerling, *Zionism and Territory*, 163.
40. Kimmerling, *Zionism and Territory*.

Chapter Four

Israel, the Fourth Geneva Convention, and The Hague Regulation: Different Takings and Approaches

International Committee of the Red Cross (ICRC), "Convention (IV) Relative to the Protection of Civilian Persons in Time of War," Article 49 states:

> Individual or mass forcible transfers, as well as deportations of protected persons from occupied territory to the territory of the Occupying Power or to that of any other country, occupied or not, are prohibited, regardless of their motive.
>
> Nevertheless, the Occupying Power may undertake total or partial evacuation of a given area if the security of the population or imperative military reasons so demand. Such evacuations may not involve the displacement of protected persons outside the bounds of the occupied territory except when for material reasons it is impossible to avoid such displacement. Persons thus evacuated shall be transferred back to their homes as soon as hostilities in the area in question have ceased.
>
> The Occupying Power undertaking such transfers or evacuations shall ensure, to the greatest practicable extent, that proper accommodation is provided to receive the protected persons, that the removals are effected in satisfactory conditions of hy-

> giene, health, safety and nutrition, and that members of the same family are not separated.
>
> The Protecting Power shall be informed of any transfers and evacuations as soon as they have taken place.
>
> The Occupying Power shall not detain protected persons in an area particularly exposed to the dangers of war unless the security of the population or imperative military reasons so demand.
>
> The Occupying Power shall not deport or transfer parts of its own civilian population into the territory it occupies.[1]

The international community has repeatedly affirmed the applicability of the Geneva Convention relative to the Protection of Civilian Persons in Time of War (Fourth Geneva Convention, 1949) to the Israeli-occupied West Bank and Gaza Strip, including East Jerusalem, and has insisted that Israel adhere to its articles. Articles of this Convention cover issues such as: measures that are to be taken by occupying armies under certain circumstances (for example Article 49, second paragraph[2]); prohibitions on the settlement of civilians from the occupier's country in occupied areas (Article 49, last paragraph); and prohibitions on transfers of populations from occupied areas; and prohibitions on collective punishment (Article 75(2)(d), 1977).[3]

As noted earlier, two documents describe, or prescribe, the international law of belligerent occupation: the "Respecting the Laws and Customs of War on Land and Its Annex: Regulations Concerning the Laws and Customs of War on Land. Annex to the Convention," 1907 (The Hague Regulations), and the "Convention (IV) Relative to the Protection of Civilian Persons in Time of War," 1949 (Fourth Geneva Convention).

As early as of September 1967, the Israeli prime minister, Levi Eshkol was informed that settling civilians in occupied territories would be in violation of international law.[4] Theodor Meron was the Israeli government's authority on international law. He was legal counsel at the Foreign Ministry. Born in Poland 1930, Meron would become a law professor at New York University, and later president of the U. N tribunal on war crimes committed in former Yugoslavia. Early on Meron wrote "that the key provision in international law, standing in the way of fulfilling the idealism of settling the"[5] cradle of Judaism[6] was the Fourth Geneva Convention on protection of civilians in time of war.

Meron emphasized that the prohibition regarding settlements is "categorical and is not conditioned on the motives or purposes of the transfer, and is aimed at preventive colonization of conquered territory by citizens of the conquering state."[7] If Israel did decide to put its citizens in the territories recently conquered, it was emphasized that it was of uttermost importance that it be done by military bodies and not civilian ones and that those settlements being temporary in nature.

Due to the fact that the Golan Heights lay outside of mandatory Palestine, Meron considered the area as "undoubtedly occupied territory and the prohibition of settlement applies."[8] In reference to the West Bank, Meron noted, that Israel argued that the area was not occupied, since the division of Palestine in 1949 were explicitly temporary. Theodor Meron believed Israel would have a problem of convincing the court of world diplomacy of its own stance and interpretations.

By issuing a legal proclamation stating that "military courts will fulfill the Geneva provisions"[9] and that when a military decree contradicted it, the Geneva convention took precedence, Israel's own actions showed recognition of that status.

On the day the Israel Defense Forces (IDF) took over the West Bank, the military commander issued a proclamation that he assumed all governmental powers in the area, and that the prevailing law would remain in force subject to any orders that he would promulgate.

The political-question doctrine has been most relevant in cases relating to the establishment of civilian settlements in the West

Bank since the Israeli government's settlement policy has been highly controversial in Israel itself and has met with a great deal of opposition on the international level. Most cases dealing with civilian settlements were brought by Palestinian landowners who contested the legality of the taking and use the land for this purpose.

In the *Beth El* case, Justice Alfred Witkon stated that he was not at all impressed with the argument that "the question before the Court is not justiciable as it is one that will be dealt with in peace negotiations and the Court does not deal with political questions that are in the government sphere." The Israeli Supreme Court distinguished between an individual's claim that his or her property was taken illegally and the legality of establishing civilian settlements in the West Bank. The *Beth El* case in the end of the 1970s was heard when intense peace negotiations were going on between Israel and Egypt. Witkon explained: "On the assumption that a person's property has been damaged or taking illegally, it is difficult to believe that the Court will refused a remedy to that person, because his right is likely to be subject of political negotiations."[10]

On the one had, the court was prepared to examine whether the individual's land had been requisitioned for security reasons and, within this argument, to examine the grounds of establishing that particular settlements were valid based on security grounds. On the other hand, as David Kretzmer in his *The Occupation of Justice* writes, "it was not prepared to consider the argument that under article 49, paragraph 6, of the Geneva Convention IV, establishing any civilian settlement in occupied territory is illegal. The main reason was that the Geneva Convention is not enforceable in Israel's domestic courts."[11]

Kretzmer also notes that "not long after the 1967 War ended, it became clear that the perception of the territories taken by the IDF in that as 'occupied territories' was incompatible with the political stance of many Israeli politicians, especially those who within a short time were referring to liberated territories."[12]

THE MOST COMMON ARGUMENTS FOR AND AGAINST THE ILLEGALITY OF SETTLEMENTS

One of the earliest voices of judicial dissent in regard to the view of the majority's interpretation of the West Bank and Gaza as occupied was Professor Julius Stone. Stone based his claims on the decision made by the League of Nations, "The Palestine Mandate," on the July 24, 1922, which stated "Whereas recognition has thereby been given to the historical connection of the Jewish people with Palestine and to the grounds for reconstituting their national home in that country."[13] The Jewish people claimed one part, Palestine, as its historic home with which it had nearly four millennia of unbroken connection. The Arabs claimed virtually the whole of the territories removed by the World War I from Turkish hegemony. These were the two claimant peoples, the Jews and the Arabs, between "whom the admittedly unsaintly dispensers of justice after World War I, the Principal Allied and Associated Powers, made the allocations that began the modern history of Palestine," according to Stone's *Israel and Palestine: Assault on the Law of Nations.* [14] The Palestine Mandate contained safeguards for civil and religious rights of the Arab inhabitants but studiously avoided referring to their political rights or political standing. Stone writes that, as in terms of the self-determination doctrine, no such right of Palestinians as a separate people were recognized during three decades of the League mandate or the first two decades of the United Nations. The name "Palestine" had not, for centuries before 1917, been referred to as a defined political, demographic, cultural, or territorial entity. In 1917, from Safed almost to Jerusalem, these were territories claimed to be part of Syria. A main argument made by Arabs in post-World War I negotiations was not that Palestinians would resent the loss of a Palestinian identity by the establishment of the Jewish national home in Palestine, but rather that they would resent severance of their connections with their fellow Syrians. President

Assad of Syria stated that "Palestine is a basic part of Southern Syria" which Yasser Arafat seemed to agree upon.[15]

The Arab leader Emir Feisal, recognized in 1919 that the concurrence of the Jewish and Arab nationalist movements had suffered similar oppressions, and thanked Chaim Weizmann and other Zionist leaders for being a "greater helper of our cause" and expressed the hope that the "Arabs may soon be in a position to make the Jews some return for their kindness."[16] Stones summarize his point that, the liberation principle applied to rival claims of the Jewish people and the Arab Nation. "It was then applied correctly, moreover, according to the facts of peoplehood as they then existed."[17] It was applied by allocating the overwhelming share of territory and resources of the whole Middle East to the Arab Nation as that nation then presented itself. "It was also applied by allocating to the Jewish people, as part of the same settlement, a fraction of the area, and that fraction was then reduced in 1922 to create Palestine what is now called State of Jordan."[18] The Palestinian Arab affinity with Jordan is deeply embedded in history, and in the consciousnesses of Jordan authorities. Lord Balfaour's Memorandum in 1919 noted that Palestine includes all the area east of Jordan. King Hussein wrote in his autobiography about the unity between Transjordan and Palestine.[19] Stone, as have many others, interprets Security Resolution 242, adopted in the aftermath of the Six-Day war, as not forcing Israel to withdraw from all territories but only to lines to be negotiated, which were then to become secure and recognized boundaries. He viewed the Soviets failure to, immediately after the Six Day War, seeking to brand Israel as the aggressor as main proof of this.[20] Stone argues the historical mandate clearly envisaged the continued entry of Jews from the wider Jewish people scattered the world over (in particular since the mandate already included Transjordan). It is not in dispute that at the very least Israel's standing in East Jerusalem, as on the West Bank, derives from what was initially a situation of belligerent occupation during hostilities. Nor is it seriously in dispute that her entry there was lawful, because it occurred in the course of self defence. Before the attack, Jordan was an unlawful belligerent occupant, the unlawfulness of whose entry in 1948 had prevented her from acquiring any lawful title, despite her purported annexation. The ouster of Jordanian forces by Israel in 1967 had three legal effects according to Stone:

1. The loss of any continued Jordanian territorial standing at all in relation to Jerusalem;
2. The Jordanian attack operated as completely unjustifiable repudiation of the Israel-Jordan General Armistice Agreement of April 3 1949, the core of which was the prohibition of "restort to military force," "aggressive action," and "warlike or hostile acts" by any "land, sea, or air forces." This repudiation released Israel from the restraints of the agreement; and
3. The entry of Israel into East Jerusalem and indeed the whole West Bank, was a lawful entry in course of self defense. In the context of the sovereignty vacuum in East Jerusalem, her lawful presence entitled her to assert full sovereignty.[21]

Stones interpretation has also been observed by *The Hague Initiative for International Cooperation* in their statement of jurists on the Israel-Palestine conflict in which it is stated that:

> Israel has, since 1967, referred to these territories (with the exception of East Jerusalem) as "occupied", and (although it has consistently denied that the law of belligerent occupation applies de jure) has voluntarily undertaken, as a matter of Government policy, to comply with the provisions of international humanitarian law applicable to occupied territories, in particular the Fourth Geneva Convention. There are, however, strong arguments (supported by leading international lawyers) that the territories over which Israel (re)gained control in June 1967 do not fall under the classic definition of military (belligerent) oc-

> cupation at all since there was no prior sovereign other than Israel over those territories (see discussion of uti possidetis juris in prior section); thus, the Fourth Geneva Convention is not obligatory on Israel as a matter of law.
>
> Jordan illegally controlled the "West Bank" between 1949 and 1967, having acquired control as a result of an illegal act of aggression. Its subsequent purported annexation of this territory was not sufficient to give it rights over this territory. In other words, Jordan had no territorial sovereignty over the "West Bank" between 1948 and 1967. As a result, when Israel defeated the Jordanian forces and regained control of this territory in June 1967, it was not a question of Israel taking control of "the territory of a High Contracting Party" [i.e., another State] within the meaning of the Fourth Geneva Convention. Professor Julius Stone, a foremost authority on the Geneva Conventions and the obligations of States in times of war, expressed the following: "But the Convention itself does not by its terms apply to these territories. For, under Article 2, the Convention applies 'to cases of . . . occupation of the territory of a High Contracting Party, by another such Party." Insofar as the West Bank at present held by Israel does not belong to any other State, the Convention would not seem to apply to it at all. This is a technical, though rather decisive, legal point.[22]

The Fourth Geneva Convention in 1949 changed the focus of the international law of belligerent occupation by giving greater attention to the rights of the population of the occupied territory; however, it did not change the notion of "occupation" itself.

As Eyal Benvenisti has stated, "The foundation upon which the entire law of occupation is based is the principle of inalienability of sovereignty through the actual or threatened use of force . . . From the principle of inalienability of sovereignty over a territory spring the constraints that international law imposes on the occupant."[23]

The purpose of the law of belligerent occupation is not only to protect civilians from the occupying army, but also, and perhaps primarily, to "safeguard the reversionary rights of the ousted sovereign." In situations like the West Bank and the Gaza Strip, in which some jurists argue, there was no ousted sovereign, there can accordingly be no question of occupation within the meaning of international humanitarian law.[24]

One main objective of the law of belligerent occupation is to accord protection to the local population while enabling the occupant to maintain the security of his forces. Stone, argues, that "the law of military occupation proceeds on a double assumption.[25] First, that it was a legitimate sovereign that was ousted from the territory by the occupant, second that the ousting power qualifies as a lawful belligerent occupant of it." It is remembered that neither Jordan nor any other state is a sovereign reversioner entitled to reenter the West Bank.

This argument resembles that of Stephen Schwebel. Advisor Schwebel, who was later the head of the International Court of Justice in the Hague, wrote in 1970 regarding Israel's case: "Where the prior holder of territory had seized that territory unlawfully, the state which subsequently takes that territory in the lawful exercise of self-defense has, against that prior holder, better title."[26]

Israel maintains that Article 49, paragraph 6, is not a prohibition against voluntary migrations, re-establishment of previously removed settlements, births of children to settlers, or construction of new homes and schools for natural community growth. Such things are not explicitly prohibited.

Israel's reasoning is that as the verb "to transfer" is not a synonym of the verb "to allow," the obligation is removed for the occupying power to actively prevent their civilians moving across boundaries. This interpretation is doubtful, according to Benvenisti, "since it seems that the purpose of the article is to protect the interests of the occupied population, rather than the population of the occupant."[27]

There are many cases of occupation that fall within the scope of the Fourth Geneva Convention. These include: East Timor, Western Sahara, Northern Cyprus, Nagorno-Karabakh (Armenia/Azerbaijan), Abkhazia, and Crimea. Israeli settlement activity has been criticized by UN bodies for violating Article 49, paragraph 6 of the Fourth Geneva Convention, while similar critique is applied by no international actor or body to these other settlement contexts where there is prima facie evidence of (state-sponsored) migration of persons into the occupied territory.

In *Settlers In Contested Lands: Territorial Disputes and Ethnic Conflict*, editors Oded Haklai and Neophytos Loizedes note that "even in territories recognized by the international community as disputed, the relevance of the legal framework provided by the Fourth Geneva Convention is frequently contested."[28] They further state that

> determining whether a settled territory should be defined as occupied is not a simple matter. First, because in so many of these conflicts, the claim to the territory is made on national grounds, sending states argue that they are retrieving what is rightfully theirs. Because the dispute is about ownership, the description of the territory as occupied is likely to be rejected by settlement sympathizers.
>
> Second, can a territory be considered occupied if it lacked an internationally recognized owner or was governed by a foreign empire before being taken by the sending state? Morocco makes the case that Western Sahara never had an independent government. When Spain retreated in 1975, it handed administrative authority to Morocco and Mauritania. The latter withdrew in 1979 and Morocco took over the whole region. Thus it can deny it occupies territories rightfully belonging to the Sawrahis.[29]

David M. Philips, says, "what distinguishes a system of 'law' from arbitrary systems of control is that similar situations are handled alike. A system where legal principles are applied only when it suits the political tastes of anti-Israel elites is one that has lost all credibility. The loose use of international law, disproportionately applied to Israel, undermines the notion that this is 'law' entitled to authoritative weight in the first place".[30]

Haklai and Loizedes write that "the kinds of strong international condemnation that Israel receives have never really been voiced in relation to Western Sahara. Settlers feature heavily in the discourse on the Israel and the Palestinians, and they are considered an essential component of any solution to that case. In the case of Western Sahara, settlers have rarely been acknowledged."[31]

The international community imposes a standard under Article 49, paragraph 6 on Israel which it does not apply to other alleged cases of occupation. The participating jurists remarked Professor Eugene Kontorovich in a recently published article on state practice concerning occupation:

> Clear patterns emerge from this systematic study of state practice. Strikingly, the state practice paints a picture that is significantly inconsistent with the prior conventional wisdom concerning Art. 49(6). First, the migration of people into occupied territory is a near-ubiquitous feature of extended belligerent occupations. Second, no occupying power has ever taken any measures to discourage or prevent such settlement activity, nor has any occupying power ever expressed opinio juris suggesting that it is bound to do so. Third, and perhaps most strikingly, in none of these situations have the international community or international organizations described the migration of persons into the occupied territory as a violation of Art. 49(6). Even in the rare cases in which such policies have met with international criticism, it has not been in legal terms. This suggests that the level of direct state involvement in "transfer" required to constitute an Art. 49(6) violation may be significantly greater than previously thought. Finally, neither international political bodies nor the new governments of previously occupied territories have ever embraced the removal of illegally transferred civilian settlers as an appropriate remedy.[32]

The Levy Commission Report which was requested by Prime Minister of Israel, as well as the Minister of Justice, writes that "as for Article 49 of the Fourth Geneva Convention, many have offered interpretations, and the predominant view appears to be that that article was indeed intended to address the harsh reality dictated by certain countries during World War II when portions of their populations were forcibly deported and transferred into the territories they seized, a process that was accompanied by a substantial worsening of the status of the occupied population."[33] The report further states that,

> this interpretation is supported by several sources: The authoritative interpretation of the International Committee of the Red Cross (IRCC), the body entrusted with the implementation of the Fourth Geneva Convention, in which the purpose of Article 49 is stated as follows: "It is intended to prevent a practice adopted during the Second World War by certain Powers, which transferred portions of their own population to occupied territory for political and racial reasons or in order, as they claimed, to colonize those territories. Such transfers worsened the economic situation of the native population and endangered their separate existence as a race."[34]

Legal scholars Professor Nicholas Rostow, Dean of Yale Law School in the United States, and Prof. Julius Stone, have both acknowledged that Article 49 was intended to prevent the inhumane atrocities carried out by the Nazis, for example, the massive transfer of people into conquered territory for the purpose of extermination, slave labor, or colonization.

To summarize this argument offered by Rostow:

> If the Geneva Convention does apply, it was not directed at the kind of activity undertaken by Israel. The argument, made notably by the late Morris Abram, who was on the U.S. staff at Nuremberg, is that Article 49 of the Geneva Convention responded to the Nazi experience and is directed at transfers of

large populations into occupied territories intended to colonize territories so as to endanger the economic situation or separate existence of the existing populations. Proponents of this view argue that the nature and extent of Israeli settlements in the West Bank do not threaten the native population and therefore would not violate the Geneva Convention even if it applied. [35]

Nicholas Rostow offers an a rather conciliatory view regarding settlements and their legal status. Rostow explains that "advocates of legality," with regard to the Israeli settlements,

> reject the applicability of the Geneva Convention on the ground that, under Article 2, the Convention applies only to occupation of the "territory of a High Contracting Party." They argue that no country has a recognized legal claim to the "occupied territories." Consequently, they are not territories "of" any contracting party, and therefore the Convention does not apply to Jewish settlement. In making this argument, advocates of legality stress that the international community did not recognize Jordan's annexation of the West Bank and that now Jordan has withdrawn its claim. However, the Israel-Palestine Authority agreements have reduced the area of occupied territory and de facto recognized that the Palestine Authority has most of the attributes of statehood required by international law. And it is also black letter international law that belligerent occupation does not depend on or affect title, sovereignty, the validity of claims or other ownership issues.[36]

Another argument Rostow offer in his article is:

> that even if the Geneva Convention applies and prohibits settlements established by the Israeli government, it does not prohibit Jewish settlements in the occupied territories. The argument is that the Palestine Mandate granted extensive rights to Jews in Palestine and that, until the final status of a particular area is resolved, there is no legal basis for barring Jews from settling there. Rather, the occupied territories are to be thought of as the unallocated remainder of the Mandate Territory, and settlement

> rights under the Mandate persist until a final allocation is made. Proponents of this argument point to Article 6 of the Mandate, which provides that "[t]he Administration of Palestine, while ensuring that the rights and position of other sections of the population are not prejudiced, shall facilitate Jewish immigration under suitable conditions and shall encourage . . . close settlement by Jews on the lands, including State lands and waste lands not required for public purposes.[37]

A third argument Rostow addresses is:

> the competing claims of Israel and the other Arab states. It cites the principle of law that, where a prior holder of territory had seized that territory unlawfully (in this case, Jordan), the state subsequently taking the territory in lawful exercise of self-defense has, against the unlawful prior holder, better title. This argument turns in part on the facts that led to the 1967 War and the conclusion that Israel acted in lawful self-defense against Egypt's blockade, Syrian attacks and provocations, and other menacing actions.[38]

A fourth argument from Rostow "is based on the historical claim of Jews to live in Palestine. Proponents of this argument, which arguably is not a legal one, trace the history of the region back to biblical times and assert that the Jews have had a continuous presence in the area and have a superior historical right to it."[39]

Rostow concludes by stating that "although not all the arguments advanced for and against legality are strong, legal arguments on both sides are durable on what are central points of contention. It therefore makes little practical sense to raise the profile of the issue of legality, for it would only add an insoluble element to what is already an extremely difficult problem."[40]

THE GENEVA CONVENTION APPLIES, BUT NOT JUSTICIABLE IN ISRAELI COURT SYSTEM?

In 1968, Professor Yehuda Blum published an article in the *Israel Law Review*, which dealt with the legal status of Israel on the West Bank.[41] Blum's main argument was that as annexation of the West Bank by Jordan in 1950 had not received international recognition, it was not the sovereign territory of another state when taken by Israel in 1967. It was therefore doubtful whether Israel should be regarded as an occupying power. He suggested that in such a situation Israel was not bound by those parts of the law of belligerent occupation whose object is to protect sovereign rights of the previous regime, though it was obliged to abide with the humanitarian aspects of belligerent occupation law.

The Israeli government openly contested application of the Geneva Convention to the situation in the West Bank. It adopted Blum's distinction between the whole corpus of belligerent occupation and those parts regarded as humanitarian law. The government's position became that while the Fourth Geneva Convention did not formally apply, the IDF would abide by its humanitarian provisions.

In addition to the provisions which shall be implemented in peacetime, the present Convention shall apply to all cases of declared war or of any other armed conflict which may arise between two or more of the High Contracting Parties, even if the state of war is not recognized by one of them.

"The Convention shall also apply to all cases of partial or total occupation of the territory of a High Contracting Party, even if the said occupation meets with no armed resistance."[42] The Israeli government's argument is based on the second paragraph of Article 2. The claim is that neither the West Bank nor Gaza was the territory of a "High Contracting Party" when occupied by Israel in 1967, therefore the Convention does not formally apply to their occupation. This point was made by Israel's Foreign Minister Moshe Dayan in a speech before the 32nd session of the UN General Assembly on March 22, 1977.[43] This was also the guided legal status of Israel's representatives in international bodies. The International Committee of the Red Cross has argued that the Geneva Convention is not concerned with the sovereignty of parties to a conflict. The Convention applies to all cases in which territory is occupied in the course of an armed conflict, irrespective of the status of that territory. In the *Beth El* case[44] Justice Moshe Landau was noncommittal on the formal applicability of the law of belligerent occupation to the situation then pertaining on the West Bank. Landau stated that the court was not going into the legal question of the applicability of the rules of international law and said that the Court have not been asked to deal with the question of whether the West Bank is to constitute as a belligerent occupation or not. The petitioners' main argument against the legality of Israeli civilian settlements in the territories was based on the final paragraph in article 49 of Geneva Convention IV that forbids transfer of part on an occupying power's civilian population to occupied territory. In the *Elon Moreh* case, Justice Landau referred to the important argument which Israel has voiced in the international arena regarding the status of the areas. Nevertheless, he refused to deal with the argument on the merits, explaining that the "scope of the hearing of the petition itself is delimited primarily by the requisition order issued by the regional commander, and the immediate source of the order is, according to all views, the powers that international law vests in the military commander of territory captured by his forces in war."[45]

Justice Witkon stated in the *Elon Moreh* case—in response to the settlers' argument that the West Bank is not occupied territory—that "had serious doubt regarding the status of the territory in question been raised," the Court would have been obliged to refer to the Foreign Ministry for an official certificate defining its status. Justice Witkon although, said that "it is an error to think . . . that the

Geneva Convention does not apply to Judea and Samaria. It applies, although, . . . it is not justiciable in this court."[46] This is the only judicial statement in which an explicit stance has been taken rejecting the government argument about the applicability of the Geneva Convention. Justice Aharon Barak provided an unequivocal ruling that the legal regime on the West Bank is based on the law of belligerent occupation.

> In the Six Day War "East" Jerusalem and Judea and Samaria were taken by the IDF. In "East" Jerusalem the "law, jurisdiction and administration of the State" were applied. The approach to Judea and Samaria was different. The law, jurisdiction, and administration of Israel were not applied in Judea and Samaria. . . . Judea and Samaria are held by Israel by way of military occupation or belligerent occupation. In the area a military government was established at the head of which is the military commander. The powers and authority of the military commander are derived from the rules of public international law that deal with belligerent occupation.[47]

David Kretzmer goes on to note that, "the Supreme Court has refused to regard Geneva Convention IV as part of customary international law enforceable in domestic courts. . . . Even assuming the Convention's applicability to the territories the court never expressed an opinion on the interpretation of the Convention's substantive provisions or on arguments that certain IDF actions are incompatible with those provisions."[48] That being said, one can argue that the Supreme Court implicitly argue that the Geneva Convention is applicable in the territories, just not in Israeli domestic courts. While former Justice Moshe Landau suggested that the general argument against the legality of settlements should be considered non-justiciable upon application of an individual to this court, the state attorney explicitly asked the Supreme Court to confirm that "from the point of view from the Geneva Convention there is nothing wrong in transferring land to settlers for their settlement needs."[49] The Supreme Court refused to do so. Justice Witkon stated that the question "is not an easy one, with no answer in international jurisprudence, however the failure to rule on the issue should not be interpreted as agreement with the attitude of either of the parties."[50] While he was in no way intimating that government settlement policy was incompatible with the Geneva Convention, he did not provide the government legal legitimization for the policy it sought from the Supreme Court.

Kretzmer says, "the law of belligerent occupation recognizes that military needs will be the major concern of every army of occupation."[51] Because

> the occupying army has control over the occupied territory the occupying army has the duty to take over the first and most basic task of every government: maintaining law and order and facilitating everyday life.
>
> Since political control over new territory must not be achieved by force but by international negotiation, the occupying power may not use the occupation as a means of changing the political status of the occupied territory. The latter principle is expressed in the restriction imposed by international law on the occupying state's power to change laws in occupied territory.[52]

In closing, the ICRC, "Convention (IV) Respecting the Laws and Customs of War on Land and Its Annex," Article 43 states: "The authority of the legitimate power having in fact passed into the hands of the occupant, the latter shall take all the measures in his power to restore, and ensure, as far as possible, public order and safety, while respecting, unless absolutely prevented, the laws in force in the country."[53]

NOTES

1. International Committee of the Red Cross (ICRC), "Convention (IV) Relative to the Protection of Civilian Persons in Time of War," Article 49, Geneva,

August 12, 1949, https://ihl-databases.icrc.org/ihl/WebART/380-600056 (accessed May 25, 2018).

2. For further reading, see, Article 49, second paragraph, at International Committee of the Red Cross (ICRC),https://ihl-databases.icrc.org/ihl/385ec082b509e76c41256739003e636d/6756482d86146898c125641e004aa3c5(accessed June 8, 2018).

3. See Article 75 at International Committee of the Red Cross (ICRC), "Practice Relating to Rule 103, Collective Punishments," https://ihl-databases.icrc.org/customary-ihl/eng/docs/v2_rul_rule103 (accessed June 2, 2018).

4. Gershom Gorenberg, *The Accidental Empire: Israel and the Birth of the Settlements, 1967-1977* (New York: Holt Paperbacks; 2007).

5. Gorenberg, *Accidental Empire, 100*

6. The West Bank is referred as cradle of Judaism due to the fact that Jewish patriarchs and matriarchs are believed to have lived, blossomed and buried there, as well as the belief of the presence of the twelve tribes of Israel doing the same. The reference of the West Bank as cradle of Judaism is used, among others, by Israeli Foreign Ministry that further explainthat many contemporary Israeli settlements have been re-established on sites which were home to Jewish communities in previous generations, in an expression of the Jewish people's deep historic and abiding connection with this land—the cradle of Jewish civilization and the locus of the key events of the Hebrew Bible. A significant number are located in places where previous Jewish communities were forcibly ousted by Arab armies or militia, or slaughtered, as was the case with the ancient Jewish community of Hebron in 1929. (Israel, Israel Ministry of Foreign Affairs, "Israeli Settlements and International Law," November 2015,http://www.mfa.gov.il/mfa/foreignpolicy/peace/guide/pages/israeli%20settlements%20and%20international%20law.aspx[accessed July 2, 2018]).

7. Gorenberg, *Accidental Empire, 101*

8. Gorenberg, *Accidental Empire, 101*

9. Gorenberg, *Accidental Empire, 101*

10. Israel, *Ayyub v. Minister of Defense*, (1978) 33 (2) P. D 113 (*Beth El* case), English summary, 9 Israel Yearbook on Human Rights (1979) 337.

11. David Kretzmer, *The Occupation of Justice: The Supreme Court of Israel and the Occupied Territories* (Albany: State University of New York Press, 2002), 22–23.

12. Kretzmer, *The Occupation of Justice*, 32.

13. Council of the League of Nations, "The Palestine Mandate," London, July 24, 1922, http://avalon.law.yale.edu/20th_century/palmanda.asp (accessed May 29, 2018).

14. Julius Stone, *Israel and Palestine: Assault on the Law of Nations* (Baltimore: Johns Hopkins University Press, 1981), 14.

15. Stone, *Israel and Palestine*, 12.

16. Stone, *Israel and Palestine*, 13.

17. Stone, *Israel and Palestine*, 17.

18. Stone, *Israel and Palestine*, 17.
19. Stone, *Israel and Palestine*, 24.
20. Stone, *Israel and Palestine*, 53.
21. Stone, *Israel and Palestine*, 118.
22. The Hague Initiative for International Cooperation (thinc). "The Hague Statement of Jurists on the Israel-Palestine Conflict," discussion paper, 2017, http://www.thinc.info/wp-content/uploads/2017/11/The-Hague-Statement_20171031.pdf (accessed May 25, 2018).
23. Eyal Benvenisti, *The International Law of Occupation*, new ed. (Princeton, NJ: Princeton University Press, 2004), 5–6.
24. Israel, Applicability of the Fourth Convention to Occupied Territories https://casebook.icrc.org/case-study/israel-applicability-fourth-convention-occupied-territories (accessed June 7, 2018).
25. Stone, *Israel and Palestine*, 119.
26. Stephen M. Schwebel, "What Weight to Conquest," *American Journal of International Law* 64, no. 2 (April 1970): 345–47.
27. Benvenisti, *International Law of Occupation*, 140.
28. *Settlers In Contested Lands: Territorial Disputes and Ethnic Conflict*, ed. Oded Haklai and Neophytos Loizedes (Stanford, CA: Stanford University Press, 2015), 13.
29. *Settlers In Contested Lands*, ed. Haklai and Loizedes, 13.
30. David M. Philips, "The Illegal Settlements Myth," *Commentary*, December 1, 2009, https://www.commentarymagazine.com/articles/the-illegal-settlements-myth/ (accessed May 26, 2018).
31. *Settlers In Contested Lands*, ed. Haklai and Loizedes, 69.
32. Eugene Kontorovich, "Unsettled: A Global Study of Settlements in Occupied Territories," September 9, 2016; rev. January 17, 2018, *Journal of Legal Analysis* (2017): Northwestern Public Law Research Paper No. 16-20, https://ssrn.com/abstract=2835908; http://dx.doi.org/10.2139/ssrn.2835908 (accessed May 26, 2018).
33. Israel, "The Levy Commission Report on the Legal Status of Building in Judea and Samaria," trans. Regavim (2014), June 21, 2012, 8, http://www.regavim.org/levy-report-translated-into-english/ (accessed May 26, 2018).
34. Israel, "The Levy Commission Report."
35. Nicholas Rostow, "Are the Settlements Illegal?" *American Interest* 5, no. 4 (March 1, 2010), https://www.the-american-interest.com/2010/03/01/are-the-settlements-illegal/ (accessed May 27, 2018).
36. Rostow, "Are the Settlements Illegal?"
37. Rostow, "Are the Settlements Illegal?"
38. Rostow, "Are the Settlements Illegal?"
39. Rostow, "Are the Settlements Illegal?"
40. Rostow, "Are the Settlements Illegal?"
41. Yehuda Zvi Blum, *The Missing Reversioner: Reflections on the Status of Judea and Samaria* (Jerusalem: Israel Law Review Association, under the aus-

pices of The Faculty of Law, Hebrew University of Jerusalem, 1968); first published in *Israel Law Review* 3, no. 2 (April 1968): 279–301.

42. ICRC, "Convention (IV) Relative to the Protection of Civilian Persons in Time of War," Article 2, https://ihl-databases.icrc.org/applic/ihl/ihl.nsf/Article.xsp?action=openDocument&documentId=C5031F972DD7E216C12563CD0051B998 (accessed May 25, 2018).

43. United Nations, Security Council, General Assembly 32nd sess.,Official Records, "Resolution 446 (1979) 22 of March 1979," S/RES/446 (1979), https://unispal.un.org/DPA/DPR/unispal.nsf/db942872b9eae454852560f6005a76fb/ba123cded3ea84a5852560e50077c2dc?OpenDocument (accessed May 27, 2018). What Moshe Dayan said in the UN was not necessarily his unofficial position. As shown by Gershom Gorenberg, in *The Accidental Empire*, Dayan was highly aware of how settling Israelis in the territories contravened international conventions. He acknowledged the problem, while dismissing it. Dayan appeared to have been the first politician that sought extraterritorial status for the settlers. For further reading see Gorenberg, *The Accidental Empire, 173*

44. Israel, *Ayyub v. Minister of Defense.*

45. Israel, High Court of Justice, *Duweikat et al. v. Government of Israel et al.*, judgment, HCJ 390/79, October 22, 1979, http://www.hamoked.org/Document.aspx?dID=1670 (accessed May 25, 2018).

46. Israel, High Court of Justice, *'Izzat Muhammad Mustafa Duweikat et 16 al. v. 1. Government of Israel 2. Minister of Defense 3. Military Commander for the Judea and Samaria Area 4. Nablus District Military Commander 5. Felix Menahem 6. Shvut Avraham*, case HCJ 390/79. September 6-October 22, 1979, 30–31, http://www.hamoked.org/files/2010/1670_eng.pdf (accessed May 25, 2018).

47. Kretzmer, *Occupation of Justice*, 40.

48. Kretzmer, *Occupation of Justice*, 43.

49. Israel, High Court of Justice, *Duweikat et al.*

50. Kretzmer, *Occupation of Justice*, 44

51. Kretzmer, *Occupation of Justice*, 57.

52. Kretzmer, *Occupation of Justice*, 57.

53. International Committee of the Red Cross (ICRC), "Convention (IV) Respecting the Laws and Customs of War on Land and Its Annex: Regulations Concerning the Laws and Customs of War on Land. Annex to the Convention: Article 43. Section 3. Military Authority Over the Territory of the Hostile State," The Hague, October 18, 1907, https://ihl-databases.icrc.org/ihl/WebART/195-200053? (accessed May 25, 2018).

Chapter Five

A Review of US Presidents' Policy vis-à-vis Israeli Settlements

The issue of Israeli settlements in areas captured 1967 has been a subject of constant friction between US administrations and Israeli government's. The conflict derive from (1) a clash of narratives (2) difference in political system. The State Department and continuous administrations of post-World war II have been trying to spread its hegemony, not only through hard power but also a value based policy based on human rights and humanitarian law. A keen element within human rights and humanitarian law has been to adhere to the basic principles and obligations as United Nations members to refrain from threat or use of force and acquisition of territory by war.[1] As such, the United States has lambasted Israel over what they view as a breach in human rights and humanitarian law. Many governments in the political sphere of Israel while adhering to such principles and praxis as noted above, have treated the territory conquered in 1967 as liberated. "The people of the book" has Jews been called. And it is not without a reason. From time immoral Jews have read, sang, remembered, told, retold, prayed, longed of a return to Zion. Jerusalem is in the Jewish Bible on 669 occasions, and Zion (which is usually referred to Jerusalem, other cases to the country of Israel) is mentioned on 154 occasions. The "territories," here in quotation marks, is a standing theme in the Hebrew Bible and Jewish traditions. This has, of course, affected, the discourse of Zionism. Although Zionism has different schools of thoughts, the main ideas competing, while also complementing each other, is between the Zionism of the workers, religious Zionism and revisionist Zionism. These three ideal types of Zionism has formed Israel through the years. Israel's first prime minister David Ben Gurion emphasized labor in his understanding of Zionism but was non-committal when it came to borders or how he viewed the future (at least until 1968[2]). "Why not mention [borders]? Because we don't know [what will happen]. If the UN stands its ground, we won't fight the UN. But if the UN doesn't act, and [the Arabs] wage war against us and we thwart them, and we then take the western Galilee and both sides of the corridor to Jerusalem, all this will become part of the state, if we have sufficient force. Why commit ourselves?"[3]

"Other Zionist leaders envisioned the establishment of a Jewish state in all of Palestine, from the Jordan River to the Mediterranean Sea."[4] Both religious Zionism and revisionist Zionism tend to view Israel differently, than the Zionism represented by the workers. As Independence Day 1967 approached, there is telling quote of Rabbi Zvi Yehuda Kook in *Israel A Concise History of a Nation Reborn:*

> The whole nation flowed into the streets to celebrate its feelings of joy . . . [But] I couldn't go out and join the rejoicing. I sat alone, and burdened. In those first hours I couldn't make my peace with what had happened, with the terrible news that the word of God in the book of the Prophets had not been fulfilled: They divided my land! . . . Where is our Hebron? Have we forgotten it? And where is our Schechem [Nablus]— have we forgotten it? And where is our Jericho- have we forgotten it? And where is the other bank of the Jordan River? Where is every clod of earth? Every piece of God's land? Do we have the right to cede even a centimeter of it? God forbid! . . . In that state, my whole body was stunned, wounded and severed into

> pieces. I couldn't celebrate- They divided my land! They divided the land of God! . . . I couldn't go outside to dance and rejoice. That is how the situation was nineteen years ago.[5]

Another explanatory factor behind differences that emerges between the US and Israel is the instability of Israel's political system versus the stability of US system. While the US is characterized by two party system, Israel has a system based on nation-wide proportional representation, and the number of seats which every list receives in the Knesset is proportional.[6] Since its foundation 1948, the country has had 20 elections. There is a lot of giving and taking in Israeli politics. Plenty of appeasement has to be made to satisfy the coalition partners to stay in the government. This has undoubted made every Israeli prime minister vulnerable to its constituencies.

Michael Wilner writes in the *Jerusalem Post*, "Every US president in the last five decades has characterized Israel's settlement enterprise as a lamentable project damaging its long term prospects for peace."[7] Wilner quotes Charles Yost, "The United States considers that the part of Jerusalem that came under the control of Israel in the June war, like other areas occupied by Israel, is governing the rights and obligations of an occupying power." Wilner goes on to say that

> Yost's successor under Gerald Ford called settlements "illegal," but the US did not vote at the time to reflect his position.
>
> While Reagan maintained US policy in opposition to settlement activity, he never sought to codify that position in the UN Security Council, where he ultimately vetoed 18 Israel-related resolutions.
>
> His successor, George H.W. Bush, a former UN ambassador, supported several resolutions on the Palestinian conflict that were condemnatory of Israel. He and his secretary of state, James Baker, repeatedly said that Israel's settlement activity was designed to predetermine terms of a deal with the Palestinians, but his position did not take the form of a UN resolution.

President Bill Clinton also maintained this policy without supporting it at the Security Council.[8]

LYNDON B. JOHNSON

In a posting on the Jewish Virtual Library website, "Lyndon Johnson Administration: Administration Alarmed by Israeli Settlement Plans," April 8, 1968, the Secretary of State Dean Rusk voiced "concerns about reports that Israel is planning to build settlements in territories it conquered in the Six-Day War and want American diplomats in Tel Aviv to relay American opposition to the idea."[9] Rusk's statement reads:

SUBJECT Israeli Settlements in Occupied Territories

> We have noted press and posts' reporting that the GOI is under increasing pressure to authorize and facilitate the establishment of civilian settlements in the occupied areas. Existing settlements in the Golan Heights, Sinai, and at Etzion were justified by the GOI as para-military encampments serving security purposes.
>
> Recent reports (Tel Avi A-716) indicate that these settlements are taking on aspects of permanent, civilian, kibbutz-like operations and some are, in fact, civilian kibbutzim with Nahal covers. Thus far, we have no information on the establishment of settlements by the 17 groups which Prime Minister Eshkol announced in the Knesset February 26 he had approved. While there was no suggestion in his statement that these groups would be associated with Nahal, we note that the groups filed applications with the GOI and it seems probable they are non-Nahal
>
> Although we have expressed our views to the Foreign Ministry and are confident there can be little doubt among GOI leaders as to our continuing opposition to any Israeli settlements in the occupied areas, we believe it would be timely and useful for the Embassy to restate in strongest terms the US position on this question.
>
> You should refer to Prime Minister Eshkol's Knesset statement and our awareness of internal Israeli pressures for settling

> civilians in occupied areas. The GOI is aware of our continuing concern that nothing be done in the occupied areas which might prejudice the search for a peace settlement. By setting up civilian or quasi-civilian outposts in the occupied areas the GOI adds serious complications to the eventual task of drawing up a peace settlement. Further, the transfer of civilians to occupied areas, whether or not in settlements which are under military control, is contrary to Article 49 of the Geneva Convention, which states "The Occupying Power shall not deport or transfer parts of its own civilian population into the territory it occupies."
>
> Finally, you should emphasize that no matter what rationale or explanation is put forward by the GOI, the establishment of civilian settlements in the occupied areas creates the strong appearance that Israel, contrary to the principle set forth in the [United Nations Security Council] UNSC Resolution and to US policy expressed in the President's speech of June 19, does not intend to reach a settlement involving withdrawal from those areas.[10]

The following paragraph is from a message from the Embassy in Israel to the US Department of State,

> Although we have expressed our views to the Foreign Ministry and are confident there can be little doubt among GOI leaders as to our continuing opposition to any Israeli settlements in the occupied areas, we believe it would be timely and useful for the Embassy to restate in strongest terms the US position on this question.
>
> You should refer to Prime Minister Eshkol's Knesset statement and our awareness of internal Israeli pressures for settling civilians in occupied areas. The GOI is aware of our continuing concern that nothing be done in the occupied areas which might prejudice the search for a peace settlement. By setting up civilian or quasi-civilian outposts in the occupied areas the GOI adds serious complications to the eventual task of drawing up a peace settlement. Further, the transfer of civilians to occupied areas, whether or not in settlements which are under military control, is contrary to Article 49 of the Geneva Convention, which states

"The Occupying Power shall not deport or transfer parts of its own civilian population into the territory it occupies."[11]

RICHARD NIXON

In a statement from Ambassador Charles Yost, U.S. Permanent Representative to the United Nations, UN Security Council, on July 1, 1969, he noted to President Nixon:

> The expropriation or confiscation of land, the construction of housing on such land, the demolition or confiscation of buildings, including those having historic or religious significance, and the application of Israeli law to occupied portions of the city are detrimental to our common interests in [Jerusalem]. The United States considers that the part of Jerusalem that came under the control of Israel in the June war, like other areas occupied by Israel, is governing the rights and obligations of an occupying Power. Among the provisions of international law which bind Israel, as they would bind any occupier, are the provisions that the occupier has no right to make changes in laws or in administration other than those which are temporarily necessitated by his security interests, and that an occupier may not confiscate or destroy private property. The pattern of behaviour authorized under the Geneva Convention of 12 August 1949 and international law is clear: the occupier must maintain the occupied area as intact and unaltered as possible, without interfering with the customary life of the area, and any changes must be necessitated by the immediate needs of the occupation.[12]

GERALD FORD

Ford's administration is most remembered for a vitally important letter.[13] David Bedein, in his article "President Ford´s Legacy for Israel," writes: "The letter, written on September 1, 1975, followed six months of American pressure on Israel to sign a peace agreement with Egypt, with which Israel was still in war. That agreement required Israel to give away important assets to Cairo - including pieces of the Sinai desert that contained valuable oil resources." Furthermore, "the letter from President Ford emphasizes the vital importance for Israel to maintain the Golan Heights. Israel had acquired the Golan Heights from Syria in 1967, following 19 years of Syrian shells on Israel's northern communities from the towering Golan Heights, and Syria's incessant attacks from Golan on the Galilee Sea—Israel's only freshwater resource, from where Israel's National Water Carrier pumps water to the whole country." Furthermore it is stated that "In the spirit of the special relationship existing between the United States and Israel and in light of the determination of both sides to avoid a situation in which the U.S. and Israel would pursue divergent courses in peace negotiations, the U.S. will take the position that these are negotiations between the parties."[14]

JIMMY CARTER

On March 23, 1976, the U.S. Ambassador to the United Nations, William W. Scranton, declared in the Security Council that Israel's settlements in the occupied territories were illegal and that its claim to all of Jerusalem was void.

Scranton said: "The United States position on the status of Jerusalem has been stated here on numerous occasions since the Arab portion of that city was occupied by Israel in 1967. . . . The future of Jerusalem will be determined only through the instruments and processes of negotiation, agreement and accommodation. Unilateral attempts to predetermine the future have no standing."[15] In an interview with President Jimmy Carter, April 12, 1980, he said:"Our position on the settlements is very clear. We do not think they are legal, and they are obviously an impediment to peace. The Israeli Government, however, feels that they have a right to those settlements. "[16]

During the administration of President Carter, the United States took the view that settlements are illegal under the Fourth Geneva Convention. Secretary of State Cyrus Vance made this clear in Congressional testimony before the House Committee on Foreign Affairs, on March 21, 1980:

> U.S. policy toward the establishment of Israeli settlements in the occupied territories is unequivocal and has long been a matter of public record. We consider it to be contrary to international law and an impediment to the successful conclusion of the Middle East peace process. . . . Article 49, paragraph 6, of the Fourth Geneva Convention is, in my judgment, and has been in the judgment of each of the legal advisers of the State Department for many, many years, to be . . . that [settlements] are illegal and that [the Convention] applies to the territories.[17]

Carter wanted to create peace between Israel and her neighbors, which involved Israeli withdrawal from territories that were captured in 1967, and to create a Palestinian entity. Menachem Begin (then Israeli Prime Minister) answered Carter that he could agree with Carter on these points except for a Palestinian entity. For Begin, the right of every Jew and Israel to settle in Judea and Samaria (the biblical name of the West Bank, frequently used by the Israeli) was legitimate. The main disagreement between Carter and Begin was the future of the West Bank. Carter said to Begin that Israeli settlements established in the territories were serious threats to peace and to the process of initiate Palestinian political rights.[18] Carter felt that all territories should be returned if it would become a fully negotiated political solution. From his perspective, Begin's ideology and settlements affected the prospect of full peace. The initial attitude towards Judea and Samaria limited the geographical substance that could be discussed in the pursuit of an agreement between Jordan or the Palestinians.

At Jimmy Carters first encounter with Israeli prime minister Menchem Begin, Begin took out a piece of paper from his pocket and said with sudden good humor, "Mr President, here in the United States of America there are eleven places named Hebron, five places named Shiloh, four places named Bethel, and six places named Bethlehem."

Carter. Indeed there are. Within twenty miles of my home there is a Bethel and a Shiloh.

Begin. May I be permitted to visit the one day?

Carter. Of course. With pleasure! There are three Baptist churches there.

Begin. In that case, I shall bring along our chief rabbi to protect me.

(Everybody laughed, but it was a hallow laugh.)

Begin. Allow me to put to you a hypothetical question. Imagine one day that the governors of the states in which these Hebrons and Shilohs and Bethels and Bethlehemes were located were to issue a decree, declaring that any citizen of the United States was free to settle in any one of these places except for one category—the Jews. Jews are forbidden to build homes in the Shilohs and the Hebrons and the Bethels and the Bethlehem of America—so it would be decreed!

(Begin threw up his hands and let out an inflated sigh)

Begin. Oh dear! Everybody is welcome to settle in any of these places except for the People of the Book. Good women, and men everywhere would cry from the rooftops—"Scandalous! Discrimination!" "Bigotry!" "Am I not right? So how can you expect me, a Jewish prime minister of the Jewish State who heads a cabinet of fifteen Jews, free men all—how can you expect me to forbid my fellow Jews from acquiring a piece of land and building a home in the original Shiloh, in the original Bethel, in the original Bethlehem and in the original Hebron, from where our Jewish forefathers originally came? Would that not be scandalous?"[19]

This story illustrate quite well the competition of narratives and the differentiation of historical truth that continues until today between Israel and its surroundings.

Carter and Moshe Dayan, like Begin, had opposite views on the settlement issue. Unlike Menachem Begin, whose view was characterized by "ideology, Dayan preferred not to encourage establishing settlements except when serving military or strategic purposes."[20]

Dayan felt Israel should settle in the territories as long as the Arabs were not forced out and as long as the Jews did not settle in the midst of them. Finally, "Israelis and Arabs would have to live side by side. Functional partition, if adopted, would result in the development and perpetuation of two types of citizens living side by side. But Dayan was pragmatic and believed that 'no matter what we [Israelis] do for them, in their eyes, we shall always be seen as conquerors.'"[21] March 22, 1979, the UN Security Council adopts Resolution 446 declaring that Israeli settlements "have no legal validity and constitute a serious obstruction to achieving a comprehensive, just and lasting peace in the Middle East." The resolution, adopted 12-0 with three abstentions, also "strongly deplores the failure of Israel to abide by" previous council resolutions critical of the settlements and calls on it to both rescind previous actions and refrain from any future actions "affecting the demographic composition of the Arab territories occupied since 1967, including Jerusalem, and, in particular, not to transfer parts of its own civilian population into the occupied Arab territories."[22]

RONALD REAGAN

President Reagan's views differed from his predecessors in stating that Israeli settlements were not illegal, but merely "unreasonable" and "unnecessary provocative." On February 2, 1981, President Reagan went against US policy that has been in place since 1967, with regard to the legality of the settlements. "As for the West Bank and settlements there, I do not agree with the former administration, which referred to them as illegal. They are not illegal."[23]

The Reagan Plan states that

> the United States will not support the use of any additional land for the purpose of settlements during the transition period [5 years after Palestinian election for a self-governing authority]. Indeed, the immediate adoption of a settlement freeze by Israel, more than any other action, could create the confidence needed for wider participation in these talks. Further settlement activity is in no way necessary for the security of Israel and only diminishes the confidence of the Arabs that a final outcome can be freely and fairly negotiated.[24]

However, some consider that Reagan understood that allegations of illegality directed against Israel's behavior in the West Bank and Gaza had no legal credibility in the sense of objective jurisprudence. Rather, it had to do with the use of law as a weapon to isolate Israel on the diplomatic front as an introduction to legitimize terrorism and other hostility to Israel as a pariah state.

For those who seek to drive a wedge in the U.S.–Israel relationship over the settlement issue, the UN Security Council is the ideal venue, a place where the Palestinians have many friends and where the Israelis have few. Reagan's ambassador to the United Nations, Jeane J. Kirkpatrick, described the Security Council thirty years ago in a way that makes plain how little has changed:

> What takes place in the Security Council more closely resembles a mugging than either a political debate or an effort at problem-solving. . . . Israel is cast as villain . . . in [a] melodrama . . . that features . . . many attackers and a great deal of verbal violence. . . . The goal is isolation and humiliation of the victim. . . . The attackers, encountering no obstacles, grow bolder, while other nations become progressively more reluctant to as-

> sociate themselves with the accused, out of fear that they themselves will become a target of bloc hostility.[25]

The Reagan formula that was repeatedly used was "settlements are not illegal."[26] An article in the *New York Times*, September 9, 1982, may provide some degree of clarity regarding the administration's ambivalence surrounding Israeli settlements. This article explains that the United States is looking for a freeze of new settlements, but that it will oppose Arab efforts to remove existing settlements.[27]

With regard to the status of the Jewish settlements, the administration said that "this must be determined during the final status negotiations."[28] But it was also established that the United States would oppose Israeli control over settlements in the future as extraterritorial outposts.

GEORGE H. W. BUSH

Reagan's successor, George H. W. Bush, took US settlement criticism one step further than did the previous administrations. His statement at a press conference: "My attitude is that US foreign policy says we do not think there should be new settlements in the West Bank or East Jerusalem" was not remarkable. The fact that Bush Sr. conditioned 10 billion dollars to Israel in exchange for a total freeze of settlements was a sign that the Republicans was serious in its efforts to thwart what many viewed as a serious impediment to peace negotiations.[29] He later compromised and allowed the loan to go ahead, but with deductions corresponding to Israel's construction in the occupied territories.

And in 1971, in a statement when he was the U.S. Ambassador to the United Nations, Bush Sr. declared: "We regret Israel's failure to acknowledge its obligations under the Fourth Geneva Convention as well as its actions which are contrary to the letter and spirit of this convention."[30]

During a news conference in March 1990, Bush Sr. said:

> My position is that the foreign policy of the United States says we do not believe there should be new settlements in the West Bank or in East Jerusalem. And I will conduct that policy as if it's firm, which it is, and I will be shaped in whatever decisions we make to see whether people can comply with that policy. And that's our strongly held view. We think it's constructive to peace—the peace process—if Israel will follow that view. And so, there's divisions in Israel on this question, incidentally. Parties are divided on it. But this is the position of the United States, and I'm not going to change that position.[31]

The president's Secretary of State James A. Baker III was as straight forward as the President himself was on this issue.

> Every time I have gone to Israel in connection with the peace process on each of my four trips, I have been met with the announcement of new settlement activity. This does violate United States policy. It's the first thing that Arab governments, the first thing the Palestinians in the territories—whose situation is really quite desperate—raise with us when we talk to them. I don't think that there is any bigger obstacle to peace than the settlement activity that continues not only unabated but at an enhanced pace.[32]

BILL CLINTON

As mentioned, President George H. W. Bush was forced to back down on the United States' "controversial the $10 billion loan guarantee to Israel." Some claim that it was due to an attack by "leading candidates—including leading candidates for the 1992 Democratic presidential nomination—[who] attacked Bush from the right by calling on the president to grant the loan guarantee unconditionally."[33]

Stephen Zunes's article goes on to say, "these predominantly Democratic critics claimed that the loans were to be used for housing for Jewish immigrants from the former Soviet Union," although "none of the money in the loan agreement was actually earmarked for such purposes."[34]

> Under pressure from the Democrats—who controlled both Congress Houses—as well as incipient Democratic presidential nominee Bill Clinton, Bush capitulated and approved the loan guarantee to Israel in July 1992, getting the Israelis to only limit new construction to the "natural growth" of existing settlements. By the following year, however, it became apparent that Israel, with the acquiescence of the new Clinton administration, interpreted this restriction so liberally that the number of new Israeli colonists in the territories grew faster than ever.
>
> When the Oslo agreements were signed in September 1993, the Palestinians pressed to address the settlements issue immediately. The Clinton administration, however, insisted on such discussions being delayed. By putting off such a fundamental issue as the settlements as a "final status question," the United States gave Israelis the ability to continue to create facts on the ground, although the peace process slowly moved forward.[35]

Jewish Telegraph Agency reports that

> Clinton did not just tolerated the expansion of settlements, but actually encouraged it. Under pressure from the peace and human rights groups, [George H. W] Bush had attached a provision to the 1992 loan guarantee agreement requiring the president to deduct the costs of further settlement from the $2 billion annual installment on the loan. In October 1993, the U.S. officially announced to Israel that there would be a $437 million deduction on loan guarantee due to settlement construction during the 1993 fiscal year. However. . . . Clinton granted Israel $ 500 million in US military supplies from NATO stocks in Europe.[36]

On the contrary President Bill Clinton did *not* ask Israeli Prime Minister Yitzhak Rabin to freeze all housing construction in settlements, including Jerusalem, in order to get the Oslo process started.

Had he made such a demand, *Rabin would have refused.* Rabin told the Knesset, "I explained to the president of the United States . . . that I wouldn't forbid Jews from building privately in the area of Judea and Samaria . . . I am sorry that within united Jerusalem construction is not more massive."[37] On January 3, 1995, in response to the Rabin government's announcement of expanded construction, the State Department spokesman said, "The parties themselves . . . have to judge whether it presents any kind of a problem in their own dialogue. The important thing is to continue to meet." The spokesman added on January 10, 1995, "We admit that settlements are a problem, but we . . . enjoin the parties to deal with these issues in their negotiations."[38] Another insightful observation is offered by the chief negotiator in Camp David talks 2000, Shlomo Ben Ami. In *Scars of War, Wounds of Peace*, Ben Ami explains that however creative and epoch-making the Oslo accords might have been, they also contained the seeds of their own destruction. An Israeli politician described them as a Swiss cheese with more holes than cheese—and essentially built on unequal relations.

> Amazing as it may sound, there is nothing in the letter of the Oslo accords that prevented the creation of settlements. The blame should be put at the door of the Palestinian negotiators who all came from Tunis and had no knowledge of the conditions on the ground. Local leaders who had been brought up under the occupation, and the arrogance and agrarian hunger of the settlers, would not have let this happen. It was this fatal symmetry between settlements and terrorism that became the hallmark of the Oslo years.[39]

In statements by Bill Clinton and George W. Bush in the *Washington Post*, it is written: "The Israeli people also must understand that . . . the settlement enterprise and building bypass roads in the heart of what they already know will one day be part of a Palestinian state is inconsistent with the Oslo commitment that both sides negotiate a compromise."[40]

GEORGE W. BUSH

On April 4, 2002, President George W. Bush, in a speech on the Middle East,says settlement activity must cease. "Consistent with the Mitchell plan, Israeli settlement activity in occupied territories must stop, and the occupation must end through withdrawal to secure and recognized boundaries, consistent with United Nations Resolutions 242 and 338."[41]

On November 19, 2003, the UN Security Council unanimously adopts Resolution 1515 endorsing the Road Map. As part of the plan's first phase, Israel "immediately dismantles settlement outposts erected since March 2001 [and] freezes all settlement activity (including natural growth of settlements)."[42] March 2001 marks the first full month in power of new Prime Minister Ariel Sharon, who presides over a period of rapid settlement growth.

On December 18, 2003, Israeli Prime Minister Ariel Sharon announces a plan for Israeli disengagement from Gaza and a dismantling of all Gaza settlements but reaffirms Israel's intent to hang onto settlements elsewhere. "Settlements which will be relocated are those, which will not be included in the territory of the State of Israel in the framework of any possible future permanent agreement. At the same time, in the framework of the Disengagement Plan, Israel will strengthen its control over those same areas in the Land of Israel which will constitute an inseparable part of the State of Israel in any future agreement."[43]

President George W. Bush played a key role in making Sharon's withdrawal from Gaza possible by softening U.S. policy on the settlement issue. To offset the concession that Sharon was making, and counter opposition to it from Israel's Right, he wrote a letter to Sharon on April 14, 2004, acknowledging that, "In light of new realities on the ground, including already existing major Israeli populations centers, it is unrealistic to expect that the outcome of final status negotiations will be a full and complete return to the armistice lines of 1949. . . . It is realistic to expect that any final status agreement will only be achieved on the basis of mutually agreed changes that reflect these realities."[44] One implication of the letter was that the United States would treat Israeli construction in communities that all parties knew will remain part of Israel in any future two-state agreement, like the Jewish neighborhoods of Jerusalem, differently from settlement activity on controversial areas in the interior of the West Bank. Elliott Abrams, the White House advisor who negotiated the Bush administration's compromises on the natural growth of settlement,explained the significance of the step Bush took last June in the *Wall Street Journal*:

> There were indeed agreements between Israel and the United States regarding the growth of Israeli settlements on the West Bank. . . . The prime minister of Israel relied on them in undertaking a wrenching political reorientation . . . the removal of every single Israeli citizen, settlement and military position in Gaza. . . . There was a bargained-for exchange. Mr. Sharon was determined to . . . confront his former allies on Israel's right by abandoning the 'Greater Israel' position. . . . He asked for our support and got it, including the agreement that we would not demand a total settlement freeze.[45]

Under Bush's remaining presidential term, the US administration, along with the Quartet, continuously castigate Israel over its settlements. But with regards to the question of Israeli settlements, he might best be remembered by acknowledging that "it is unrealistic to expect that the outcome of final status negotiations will be a full and complete return to the armistice lines of 1949."[46]

BARACK OBAMA

President Barack Obama apparently believed that pressuring Israel to halt construction of homes in Jewish neighborhoods in parts of Jerusalem that had been formerly controlled by Jordan would advance peace. In reality, the opposite ensued. As a result, he was the first president since the Madrid conference in 1991 to have had no sustained high-level, direct negotiations between the parties.

Obama's failure to distinguish construction in east Jerusalem from settlement activity in the West Bank put him at odds with the Israeli consensus. No major party in Israel, and no significant part of the Jewish public, are willing to count the Jewish neighborhoods that fall within the juridical boundaries of Jerusalem as "settlements" to be "frozen." Moreover, the concept of agreed settlement blocs laid the basis for a compromise between the Israeli and American governments. Obama's policy shift moved the settlement issue out of the realistic zone of compromise: his rejection of the Bush policy of treating the "settlement blocs" differently from the "non-consensus" settlements deeper in the West Bank interior. The special status of the blocs arose from the Camp David peace talks in July 2000, at which Yasser Arafat accepted President Clinton's proposal that certain bedroom suburbs of Tel Aviv and Jerusalem, comprising only 5 percent of the land of the West Bank but including about 80 percent of the settlers, would come under Israeli sovereignty. In exchange, Israel would "swap" land from its own pre-1967 territory. Israel would relinquish settlements outside the blocs, but retain the settlement blocs themselves. The understandings reached at Camp David had no legal standing after the negotiations collapsed in 2001, but the concept of agreed settlement blocs laid the basis for a compromise between the succeeding Israeli and American governments.

Israel understood the agreement made between Ariel Sharon and George W. Bush as the United States would treat settlements in the blocs that would remain part of sovereign Israel in a future negotiation differently from settlements outside the blocs agreed upon at Camp David. The government of Israel believed it had a commitment from the United States to accept that a "freeze on natural growth" would *not* apply to construction inside these blocs, provided that it remained within the territorial limits set forth at Camp

David. Sharon's successor, Ehud Olmert, stated this publicly in April 2008. "It was clear from day one to Abbas, Rice and Bush that construction would continue in population concentrations—the areas mentioned in Bush's 2004 letter. . . . I say this again today: Beitar Illit will be built, Gush Etzion will be built; there will be construction in Pisgat Ze'ev and in the Jewish neighborhoods in Jerusalem. It's clear that these areas will remain under Israeli control in any future settlement."[47]

Secretary of State Hillary Clinton denied that the Obama administration was bound by any such understanding. "That was an understanding that was entered into, so far as we are told, orally. That was never made a part of the official record of the negotiations, as it was passed on to our administration. . . . Nobody in a position of authority at the time that the Obama administration came into office said anything about it. And in fact, there is also a record that President Bush contradicted even that oral agreement."[48]

Israelis were bitterly disappointed by the Obama administration's refusal to acknowledge agreements made with a prior U.S. government that the Israelis considered vital and binding.

Led by former Senate Majority Leader George J. Mitchell, the Obama peace team was seized with the idea of a settlement "freeze" as a confidence-building measure to the reluctant Palestinians and bring them back to the negotiating table.

In an effort to placate Obama, in November 2009, Prime Minister Benjamin Netanyahu announced a ten-month freeze on construction permits for new residences and the start of any new residential construction in the settlements.

For nine of the ten months of the freeze, Netanyahu's concession did not have the intended effect. For all but the last month, Mahmoud Abbas refused to resume negotiations, even with the freeze, saying it fell short of the total freeze in Jerusalem that President Obama had promised him. "At first, President Obama stated in

Cairo that Israel must stop all construction activities in the settlements. Could we demand less than that?" Mitchell later said, "The real loss was that we didn't get a full ten months. We didn't get nine months or eight months. We got one month—less than a month, and it was not enough time to gain traction and get the parties invested in continuing the process."[49] According to the Israeli Arab journalist Khaled Abu Tomeh the issue of the settlements became a "major obstacle to peace" only when President Barack Obama one day demanded that Israel freeze all settlement activities.[50] Obama's demand embarrassed the Palestinian Authority, whose leaders rushed to endorse the call. The Palestinian Authority leadership even took a step further by announcing that it would not return to the negotiating table unless Israel halted all settlement activities.

Before his speech in Cairo, President Obama was firm in his opposition to Israeli settlements. In aspeech in Cairoon June 4, 2009, he states that Washington "does not accept the legitimacy of continued Israeli settlements. . . . It is time for these settlements to stop."[51]

Obamas presidency made it more clear than any US President before him that Israeli settlement policies was of major concern. In February 18, 2011, fourteen of the Security Council's fifteen members backed a resolution put forward by the Palestinian Authority condemning the construction of Israeli settlements. But the resolution is defeated by a US veto.[52] Washington says Israeli-Palestinian differences should be resolved only through direction negotiations between the parties and without Security Council interference. Susan Rice, US Ambassador to the United Nations, says the veto should not be construed as American support for new Israeli settlements.

In a speech May 19, 2011, at the US Department of State, President Obama says "We believe the borders of Israel and Palestinian should be based on the 1967 lines with mutually agreed [land] swaps, so that secure and recognized borders are established for both states."[53] A day later, Netanyahu meets with Obama and rules out a reliance on the pre-1967 lines, saying this would undermine Israel's viability.[54]

With the Obama administration abstaining Resolution 2334, adopted on December 23, 2016, there was a firm condemnation of the Israeli government's policy on the settlements. Nonetheless the resolution was adopted under chapter 6 of the United Nations Charter, and does not include sanctions to be imposed on Israel for failure to implement it.[55]

A key motif in the resolution, as emphasized in paragraph 4, is the need to cease all activity concerning the settlements in order to salvage the two-state solution. The preamble to the resolution condemns "all measures aimed at altering the demographic composition, character and status of the Palestinian Territory occupied since 1967, including East Jerusalem" and expresses "grave concern that continuing Israeli settlement activities are dangerously imperilling the viability of the two-State solution based on the 1967 lines."[56] The resolution stipulates that measures should be taken "to reverse the negative trends on the ground which are steadily eroding the two-State solution and entrenching a one-State reality."

The resolution contains clauses that already appear in Security Council Resolutions 446, 452, and 465 from 1979–1980. The wording is also reminiscent of a 2011 resolution initiated by the Palestinians on the subject of the settlements, which the United States vetoed. At the same time, the resolution also contains new clauses that did not appear in previous documents.

The resolution states that the settlements in the occupied Palestinian territories, including East Jerusalem, have "no legal validity" and are "a flagrant violation of international law and a major obstacle to the achievement of the two-State solution and a just, lasting and comprehensive peace" (paragraph 1). The preamble to the resolution also states that as an occupying power, Israel is obligated to abide by its legal obligations under the Fourth Geneva Convention.

An interesting assessment is made by the think tank *The Institute for National Security Studies* (INSS).[57] While the resolution does not distinguish between remote isolated settlements, settlement blocs, and East Jerusalem, nor between construction on state-owned land and construction on privately owned land, the recurring emphasis in the resolution that settlement activity obstructs the possible achievement of the two-state solution indicates that in practice, there would be a difference in the possible response to a violation of the resolution by construction activity in the settlement blocs compared to construction deep within the territory or the seizure of Palestinian private land for the purpose of establishing settlements. Assertions that Israel is in any case regarded as being in violation of international law, and that such distinctions are therefore meaningless, are mistaken. As in any legal system, there is a difference in the response to acts of varying degrees of severity. One can therefore reasonably estimate that if Israel's settlement activities are more restrained and relieve international anxiety about obstruction of a two-state solution, the risk that the resolution will lead to actual measures harmful to Israel will be reduced significantly.

The resolution underlines that the Security Council "will not recognize any change to the 4 June 1967 lines, including with regard to Jerusalem, other than those agreed by the parties through negotiations" (paragraph 3). Such a provision was not included in previous resolutions and proposals. This formulation is more restrictive than the wording in Resolution 242 from 1967 that is the agreed basis for the permanent status agreement, which refers to "secure and recognized boundaries."[58] Furthermore, in previous draft proposals that tried to set parameters for ending the conflict (such as the 2014 Jordanian proposal and the 2015 French proposal), the 1967 lines were referred to as reference lines for determining borders "with land swaps." According to Resolution 2334, the point of departure is solely the 1967 lines. Any demand for setting a different boundary, including through land swaps, will be referred to as an Israeli demand that deviates from what is stated in the resolution. Accordingly, although the resolution recognizes the possibility of negotiated agreement on other lines, this paragraph will possibly serve the Palestinian side as a bargaining chip in negotiations. In addition, the wording of this paragraph, which emphasizes agreement through negotiations, might be interpreted as preventing recognition of borders set through unilateral measures, even in a situation in which Israel is willing to withdraw from large sections of the territories to settlement blocs, and even if Palestinian obduracy prevents any possibility of formulating an agreement through negotiations.

> The resolution calls upon all states to distinguish "between the territory of the State of Israel and the territories occupied since 1967" (paragraph 5). This paragraph, which did not appear in previous formulations, is liable to lead to the escalation of already existing measures aimed at boycotting products from the settlements, and to demands that businesses refrain from activity in the territories (including East Jerusalem) as a condition for transactions with them. The provision might also serve as a basis for efforts to institute civil court proceedings in various countries against parties that do not comply with this demand. On the other hand, this provision does make the point that there are no grounds for boycotting the State of Israel—only the settlements.[59]

It is stated explicitly that the Security Council "will not recognize any change to the 4 June 1967 lines, including with regard to Jerusalem, other than those agreed by the parties through negotiations."[60] If one takes a closer reading of UNSC Resolution 242 adopted in the aftermath of the Six-Day War, it is clear that the wording, interpretation, and end goal is different. The UNSC 242 famously called for “Withdrawal of Israel armed forces from territories occupied in the recent conflict.” The British delegation, which drafted the resolution, specifically said they omitted a “the” before “territories” to leave the extent of the required withdrawal open for future negotiation. Indeed, in earlier drafts, the United Kingdom and the United States rejected attempts by the Arab-Soviet aligned nations to explicitly require withdrawal from “all” or “the” territories. The Western states insisted that it would be both unreasonable and unrealistic to require a complete Israeli withdrawal to the arbitrary 1949 Armistice Lines, which would also entail a complete Israeli abandonment of Jerusalem’s holy sites.

The discussion concerning the consequences of Resolution 2334 is quite interesting. A closer reading of the resolution makes it clear that it was a hasty work, both historically and present time, which might open up for unintended repercussions: (1) Discrepancy between private ownership and the political position made by UNSC; and (2) The discrepancy between bilateral agreements and multilateral agreements.

DONALD TRUMP

Ahead of the vote in the UNSC regarding Resolution 2334, “Israel, it was widely reported at the time, had been lobbying the team of then President-elect Trump in an attempt to derail the vote.”[61] Donald Trump’s former national security advisor, Michael Flynn, has admitted trying to get Russia to block a critical UN resolution—and an Israeli official stated they sought Trump’s help. “Among the statements about which Flynn has admitted lying to the FBI is his depiction of a conversation with the then Russian ambassador, Sergey Kislyak, relating to the run-up to the controversial December 2016 UN security council resolution 2334 on Israeli settlement building—which passed after the Obama administration abstained.”[62]

The current United States Ambassador to the United Nations, Nikki Haley, made the following remarks on Resolution 2334:

> This week marks the one-year anniversary of the passage of Resolution 2334. On that day, in this Council, in December 2016, the United States elected to abstain, allowing the measure to pass. Now it's one year and a new administration later. Given the chance to vote again on Resolution 2334, I can say with complete confidence that the United States would vote "no." We would exercise our veto power. The reasons why are very relevant to the cause of peace in the Middle East.
>
> On the surface, Resolution 2334 described Israeli settlements as impediments to peace. Reasonable people can disagree about that, and in fact, over the years the United States has expressed criticism of Israeli settlement policies many times.
>
> But in truth, it was Resolution 2334 itself that was an impediment to peace. This Security Council put the negotiations between Israelis and the Palestinians further out of reach by injecting itself, yet again, in between the two parties to the conflict. By misplacing the blame for the failure of peace efforts squarely on the Israeli settlements, the resolution gave a pass to Palestinian leaders who for many years rejected one peace proposal after another. It also gave them encouragement to avoid negotiations in the future. It refused to acknowledge the legacy of failed negotiations unrelated to settlements. And the Council passed judgment on issues that must be decided in direct negotiations between the parties.
>
> If the United Nations' history in the peace efforts proves anything, it is that talking in New York cannot take the place of face-to-face negotiations between the regional parties. It only sets back the cause of peace, not advance it.
>
> As if to make this very point, Resolution 2334 demanded a halt to all Israeli settlement activity in East Jerusalem— even in the Jewish Quarter of the Old City. This is something that no responsible person or country would ever expect Israel would do. And in this way, Resolution 2334 did what President Trump's announcement on Jerusalem as the capital of Israel did

> not do: It prejudged issues that should be left in final status negotiations.
>
> Given the chance today, the United States would veto Resolution 2334 for another reason. It gave new life to an ugly creation of the Human Rights Council: the database of companies operating in Jewish communities. This is an effort to create a blacklist, plain and simple. It is yet another obstacle to a negotiated peace. It is a stain on America's conscience that we gave the so-called BDS movement momentum by allowing the passage of Resolution 2334.
>
> To the United Nations' shame, this has been a disproportionately hostile place for the Middle East's most enduring democracy.
>
> The United States refuses to accept the double standard that says we are not impartial when we stand by the will of the American people by moving our US embassy, but somehow the United Nations is a neutral party when it consistently singles out Israel for condemnation.
>
> For decades, Israel has withstood wave after wave of bias in the UN and its agencies. The United States has often stood beside Israel. We did not on December 23, 2016. We will not make that mistake again.
>
> This week marks the one year anniversary of a significant setback for Middle East peace. But the United States has an undiminished commitment to helping bring about final status negotiations that will lead to lasting peace.
>
> Our hand remains extended to both parties. We call on all countries that share this commitment to learn the hard lessons of the past and work to bring Israel and the Palestinian people in good faith to the peace table.[63]

In his first on-camera interview since taking up his position, U.S. Ambassador to Israel David Friedman declared that only 2 percent of the West Bank is occupied and that settlements are part of Israel. A reporter is asking David Friedman about his position on the settlements in which Friedman replies:

> I think the settlements are part of Israel. I think that was always the expectation when Resolution 242 was adopted in 1967. It was, and it remains today, the only substantive resolution that was agreed to by everybody. I think the idea there, the idea was that Israel would be entitled to secure borders. The existing borders, the 1967 borders, were viewed by everybody as not secured borders, so Israel would retain a meaningful portion of the West Bank, and it would return that which it wouldn´t need for peace and security. So there was always supposed to be some notion of expansion into the West Bank but not necessarily expansion to the entire West Bank and I think that is exactly what Israel has done. I mean they are only occupying 2 % of the West Bank so I think that is consistent with Resolution 242 and that´s been the basis for 50 years for the parties to proceed. Obviously, there is important security considerations to those settlements. There are important nationalistic, historical, religious significance to those settlements. And I think the settlers view themselves as Israelis and Israel views the settlers as Israelis and I think those are the facts.[64]

Under Donald Trump's administration, Israel announced it will curb construction in West Bank settlements. Raphael Ahren and *TOI* Staff, in their essay say, "The Prime Minister's office said any future construction would be limited to existing settlement boundaries or adjacent to them. However, if legal, security or topographical limitations do not allow adherence to those guidelines, new homes will be built outside the current settlement boundaries but as close as possible to them." The White House, under Donald Trump's administration, has stated that while it did not view settlements as an obstacle to peace, "further unrestrained settlement activity does not help advance peace."[65]

NOTES

1. United Nations. Chapter I: Purposes and Principles, Article 2 (4) and paragraphs (1), (2), and (3) of the same article. http://www.un.org/en/sections/un-charter/chapter-i/index.html(accessed June 9, 2018).

2. Benny Morris,"How David Ben-Gurion Felt about the Size of the 'Tablecloth,'" Mosaic Magazine, April 9, 2018, https://mosaicmagazine.com/response/2018/04/how-david-ben-gurion-felt-about-the-size-of-the-tablecloth/ (accessed June 9, 2018).

3. Martin Kramer," The May 1948 Vote that Made the State of Israel," Mosaic Magazine, April 2, 2018 https://mosaicmagazine.com/essay/2018/04/the-may-1948-vote-that-made-the-state-of-israel/(accessed June 9, 2018).

4. Kramer, "The May 1948 Vote that Made the State of Israel."

5. Daniel Gordis, *A Concise History of a Nation Reborn* (HarperCollins, USA: NY, 2016), 261.

6. The Electoral System in Israel, https://knesset.gov.il/description/eng/eng_mimshal_beh.htm(accessed June 9, 2018)

7. Michael Wilner, "US Consistent Against Settlements—And Against UN as Appropriate Venue," *Jerusalem Post, Analysis*, December 25, 2016, http://www.jpost.com/Israel-News/Politics-And-Diplomacy/Analysis-US-consistent-against-settlements-and-against-UN-as-appropriate-venue-476504 (accessed May 27, 2018).

8. Wilner, "US Consistent Against Settlements."

9. Jewish Virtual Library, "Lyndon Johnson Administration: Administration Alarmed by Israeli Settlement Plans," April 8, 1968, http://www.jewishvirtuallibrary.org/administration-alarmed-by-israeli-settlement-plans-april-1968 (accessed May 25, 2018).

10. Jewish Virtual Library, "Lyndon Johnson Administration."

11. United States, National Archives and Records Administration, "Airgram From the Department of State to the Embassy in Israel," RG 59, Foreign Relations of the United States, 1964-1968, vol. 20, Arab-Israeli Dispute, 1967–1968, doc. 137, https://history.state.gov/historicaldocuments/frus1964-68v20/d137 (accessed June 3, 2018). For the complete text of Article 49, see International Committee of the Red Cross (ICRC). "Convention (IV) Relative to the Protection of Civilian Persons in Time of War." Geneva. August 12, 1949. https://ihl-databases.icrc.org/applic/ihl/ihl.nsf/Treaty.xsp?action=openDocument&documentId=AE2D398352C5B028C12563CD002D6B5C (accessed May 25, 2018).

12. Charles Yost, July 1, 1969 in a letter to Richard Nixon, quoted in "U.S. Ambassador's Statement in the Security Council," in *The Jerusalem Question and Its Resolution: Selected Documents*, edited by Ruth Lapîdôt and Moshe Hirsch (Dordrecht, Boston and London: Martinus Nijhoff; Jerusalem Institute for Israel, 1994), 237.

13. David Bedein, "President Ford´s Legacy for Israel," *Behind: Israel Resource Review*. January 2, 2007, http://israelbehindthenews.com/president-fords-legacy-for-israel/5187 (accessed May 25, 2018).

14. Bedein, "President Ford´s Legacy for Israel."

15. William W. Scranton, "Excerpts From Scranton's U.N. Speech," *New York Times*, March 25, 1976, http://www.nytimes.com/1976/03/25/archives/excerpts-from-scrantons-un-speech.html (accessed May 26, 2018).

16. American President Project, "Interview with the President Jimmy Carter, Question-and-Answer Session With Foreign Correspondents," April 12, 1980, http://www.presidency.ucsb.edu/ws/?pid=33269 (accessed May 24, 2018).

17. Secretary of State Cyrus Vance, before the U.S. House Committee, March 21, 1980, quoted in George J. Mitchell, *The Negotiator: A Memoir* (New York: Simon & Schuster, 2015), 234.

18. Kenneth W. Stein, *Heroic Diplomacy: Sadat, Kissinger, Carter, Begin and the Quest for Arab Israeli Peace* (New York: Routledge, 1999), 201.

19. Yehuda Avner, *The Prime Ministers: An Intimate Narrative of Israeli Leadership* (New Milford, CT: Toby Press, 2010), 423–24.

20. Stein, *Heroic Diplomacy*, 209.

21. Stein, *Heroic Diplomacy*, 234.

22. United Nations, Security Council. General Assembly 32nd sess.,Official Records, "Resolution 446 (1979) 22 of March 1979," S/RES/446 (1979), https://unispal.un.org/DPA/DPR/unispal.nsf/db942872b9eae454852560f6005a76fb/ba123cded3ea84a5852560e50077c2dc?OpenDocument (accessed May 27, 2018).

23. Bernard Gwertzman, "State Department; About the "West Bank and the Emperor's Clothes," *New York Times*, August 25, 1983, D2, http://www.nytimes.com/1983/08/25/us/state-departmt-about-the-west-bank-and-the-emperor-s-clothes.html (accessed May 25, 2018).

24. Ronald Reagan, Presidential Library, "Address to the Nation on United States Policy for Peace in the Middle East," KNBC-TV, Burbank, CA, September 1, 1982, https://www.reaganlibrary.archives.gov/archives/speeches/1982/90182d.htm (accessed May 26, 2018).

25. Jeane J. Kirkpatrick, "U.N. 'Mugging' Fails," *New York Times*, March 31, 1983, A23, http://www.nytimes.com/1983/03/31/opinion/un-mugging-fails.html (accessed May 26, 2018).

26. Jewish Virtual Library, "Ronald Reagan (1911–2004)," 2008, https://www.jewishvirtuallibrary.org/ronald-reagan (accessed May 25, 2018).

27. Ronald Reagan, "Reagan Outlines His Stands on Jewish Settlements," *New York Times*, September 9, 1982, A10, http://www.nytimes.com/1982/09/09/world/reagan-outlines-his-stand-on-jewish-settlements.html (accessed May 26, 2018).

28. Reagan, "Reagan Outlines His Stands on Jewish Settlements."

29. Yair Rosenberg, "The Most Anti-Israel President," *Tablet Magazine*, April 10, 2012, http://www.tabletmag.com/jewish-news-and-politics/96492/the-most-anti-israel-president (accessed May 27, 2018).

30. David Ignatius, "Obama on Israeli Settlements," *Washington Post*, June 4, 2009, http://www.washingtonpost.com/wp-dyn/content/article/2009/06/03/AR2009060303241.html (accessed May 25, 2018).

31. American President Project, "George Bush, The President's News Conference Following Discussions With Prime Minister Toshiki Kaifu of Japan in Palm Springs, California," March 3, 1990, http://www.presidency.ucsb.edu/ws/?pid=18215 (accessed May 24, 2018).

32. Thomas L. Friedman, "Baker Cites Israel For Settlements," *New York Times*, May 23, 1991, A5, http://www.nytimes.com/1991/05/23/world/baker-cites-israel-for-settlements.html (accessed May 25, 2018).

33. Stephen Zunes, "How Clinton and the Democrats Made Possible Israel's Settlements Expansion," *Huffington Post*, July 16, 2009, http://www.huffingtonpost.com/stephen-zunes/how-clinton-and-the-demoс_b_212292.html (accessed May 27, 2018).

34. Zunes, "How Clinton and the Democrats Made Possible Israel's Settlements Expansion."

35. Zunes, "How Clinton and the Democrats Made Possible Israel's Settlements Expansion."

36. Jewish Telegraph Agency, "U.S. Will Deduct $437 Million in Loans Because of Settlements," October 5, 1993, http://archive.jta.org/1993/10/05/archive/u-s-will-deduct-437-million-in-loans-because-of-settlements (accessed May 25, 2018).

37. Steven J. Rosen, "Obama's Foolish Settlements Ultimatum," *Middle East Forum*, April 1, 2010, http://www.meforum.org/2630/obama-settlements-ultimatum (accessed May 26, 2018).

38. Steven J. Rosen, "Israeli Settlements, American Pressure, and Peace," *Jewish Political Studies Review* 24, nos. 1–2 (Spring 2012): 32–44, http://jcpa.org/wp-content/uploads/2012/07/Rosen.pdf (accessed May 26, 2018).

39. Shlomo Ben Ami, *Scars of War, Wounds of Peace: The Israeli-Arab Tragedy* (Oxford: Oxford University Press, 2007), 212.

40. Bill Clinton and George W. Bush. "U.S. Presidential Statements on Settlements," *Washington Post*, January 7, 2001 and April 4, 2002, posted online May 23, 2009, http://www.washingtonpost.com/wp-dyn/content/article/2009/05/23/AR2009052301871_2.html (accessed May 27, 2018).

41. Chicago Tribune, "Bush Speech Excerpts," *Chicago Tribune*, April 5, 2002, http://articles.chicagotribune.com/2002-04-05/news/0204050329_1_responsible-palestinian-leaders-palestinian-authority-middle-east (accessed May 25, 2018).

42. BBC News, "The roadmap: full text", April 30, 2003,http://news.bbc.co.uk/2/hi/middle_east/2989783.stm(accessed June 9, 2018).

43. Israel, Ministry of Foreign Affairs, "Address by PM Ariel Sharon at the Fourth Herzliya Conference," December 18, 2003, www.mfa.gov.il/mfa/pressroom/2003/pages/address%20by%20pm%20ariel%20sharon%20at%20the%20fourth%20herzliya.aspx (accessed May 26, 2018).

44. Israel, Ministry of Foreign Affairs, "Exchange of letters between PM Sharon and President Bush," April 14, 2004, http://www.mfa.gov.il/mfa/foreign-policy/peace/mfadocuments/pages/exchange%20of%20letters%20sharon-bush%2014-apr-2004.aspx (accessed June 9, 2018).

45. Elliott Abrams, "Hillary Is Wrong About the Settlements," *Wall Street Journal*, June 26, 2009, https://www.wsj.com/articles/SB124588743827950599 (accessed May 24, 2018).

46. Israel, Ministry of Foreign Affairs, "Exchange of letters between PM Sharon and President Bush," April 14, 2004, www.mfa.gov.il/mfa/foreignpolicy/peace/mfadocuments/pages/exchange%20of%20letters%20sharon-bush%2014-apr-2004.aspx (accessed June 9, 2018).

47. Glenn Kessler, "Israelis Claim Secret Agreement With U.S.: Americans Insist No Deal Made on Settlement Growth," *Washington Post*, April 24, 2008, http://www.washingtonpost.com/wp-dyn/content/article/2008/04/23/AR2008042303128_pf.html (accessed May 26, 2018).

48. ABC News, "Clinton Denies Bush Agreement With Israel on Settlement," *ABC News* (blog), June 14, 2009, https://abcnews.go.com/ThisWeek/Politics/story?id=7775502&page=1 (accessed June 9, 2018).

49. Steven J. Rosen, Middle East Forum, Israeli settlements, American Pressure, and Peace", https://www.meforum.org/articles/2012/israeli-settlements,-american-pressure,-and-peace (accessed June 9, 2018).

50. Khaled Abu Tomeh, "Are Settlements the Major Obstacle to Peace?" *Gatestone Institute*, April 12, 2012, https://www.gatestoneinstitute.org/3008/settlements-obstacle-to-peace (accessed June 3, 2018).

51. Barack Obama, "Text: Obama's Speech in Cairo," *New York Times*, June 4, 2009, http://www.nytimes.com/2009/06/04/us/politics/04obama.text.html?mcubz=3 (accessed May 26, 2018).

52. United Nations, Security Council 6484th Meeting, "Security Council Fails to Adopt Text Demanding That Israel Halt Settlement Activity as Permanent Member Casts Negative Vote," SC/10178, February 18, 2011, https://www.un.org/press/en/2011/sc10178.doc.htm (accessed June 9, 2018).

53. Obama White House Archives, "Remarks by the President on the Middle East and North Africa," Office of the Press Secretary, May 19, 2011, https://obamawhitehouse.archives.gov/the-press-office/2011/05/19/remarks-president-middle-east-and-north-africa (accessed May 26, 2018).

54. Obama White House Archives, "Remarks by President Obama and Prime Minister Netanyahu of Israel After Bilateral Meeting," Office of the Press Secretary, May 20, 2011, https://obamawhitehouse.archives.gov/the-press-office/2011/05/20/remarks-president-obama-and-prime-minister-netanyahu-israel-after-bilate (accessed June 3, 2018).

55. See United Nations, *Charter of the United Nations*, June 26, 1945, http://www.un.org/en/charter-united-nations/index.html (accessed May 25, 2018).

56. United Nations S/RES/2334 (2016) Security Council, December 23, 2016, http://www.un.org/webcast/pdfs/SRES2334-2016.pdf (accessed June 3, 2018).

57. Pnina Sharvit Baruch, "Security Council Resolution 2234: Legal Significance," *IISS*, Insight No. 883, December 30, 2016, http://www.inss.org.il/publication/security-council-resolution-2334-legal-significance/ (accessed May 27, 2018).

58. Pnina Sharvit Baruch, "Security Council Resolution 2234: Legal Significance."

59. Pnina Sharvit Baruch, "Security Council Resolution 2234: Legal Significance."

60. Pnina Sharvit Baruch, "Security Council Resolution 2234: Legal Significance."

61. Peter Beaumont, "Were Other Trump Aides Lobbying for Israel Illicitly Alongside Michael Flynn?" *Guardian*, December 1, 2017, https://www.theguardian.com/us-news/2017/dec/01/michael-flynn-israel-lobbying-russia-united-nations (accessed May 25, 2018).

62. Beaumont, "Were Other Trump Aides Lobbying for Israel Illicitly Alongside Michael Flynn?"

63. *TOI* Staff, "Full text of Nikki Haley's 2 speeches at UN Security Council debate on Jerusalem," *Times of Israel*, December 18, 2017, last updated December 19, 2017, https://www.timesofisrael.com/full-text-of-nikki-haleys-speech-at-un-security-council-debate-on-jerusalem/ (accessed May 27, 2018).

64. United States, Ambassador to Israel: Interview with Israeli Walla, "The Administration Will Present the Peace Plan Within a Few Months," Walla News Channel, September 28, 2017, https://news.walla.co.il/item/3100410 (accessed May 27, 2018).

65. Raphael Ahren and *TOI* Staff, "Israel Will Curb Settlement Expansion to Satisfy Trump," *Times of Israel*, March 31, 2017, https://www.timesofisrael.com/israel-says-it-will-curb-settlement-expansion-to-satisfy-trump/ (accessed May 24, 2018).

Chapter Six

A Paradigm Shift?

On February 6, 2017, the Knesset (Israel's Parliament) passed a law for the regulation of land in Judea and Samaria (the West Bank). Land subject to the regulation is defined as that on which Israeli settlements were built "in good faith" or "with the consent of the state."

The law marked the most significant potential change to the treatment of property in the West Bank over the last forty years.[1] The government was forced to explain in writing by February 25, 2018, why it has not struck down the Settlement Regulations Law, which authorizes settler homes to be illegally built on private Palestinian property, while offering to compensate the Palestinian landowners.

The High Court of Justice has stated that it planned to hear the case before nine judges, the broadest possible legal panel, which expedites the proceedings, said representatives for both the plaintiffs and the defendants.

The law provides for the registration of land ownership under the name of the government official in charge, where ownership has not otherwise been established. Additionally, it provides for the expropriation of the rights of use and possession of privately-owned land in the region. Such expropriation will be in effect until a political resolution on the status of the region is achieved. Landowners whose property rights have been affected will be compensated. The Law for the "Regulation of Settlement in Judea and Samaria, 5777–2017,"[2] was passed with the support of sixty members with fifty-two objecting.[3] The law allows for monetary compensation to be paid to Palestinian owners for the expropriation of their lands at the rate of 125% of appropriate yearly usage fees as determined by an assessment committee, or compensation via allocation of alternative land.[4] The law provides that the assessment committee will be appointed by the Minister of Justice, in consultation with the Minister of Defense, and will include a representative from the Ministry of Justice, from the Ministry of the Treasury, and from the military.[5] A decision by the assessment committee can be appealed to an appellate committee.[6] The explanatory notes of the law[7] describe that in many cases settlements were built with the consent, the encouragement, and the participation of the state. In other cases, settlements were built by Israeli citizens "in good faith" and without the knowledge that the land on which the settlements were built was privately owned. Accordingly, "leaving the situation in these settlements as it is today or destroying them might cause difficult and unjustified harm to those who have resided in them for many years." An interesting observation is made by Israeli Democracy Institute: the further Israel advances the settlements, when the settlements are done with very generous state support, the harder it will be for Israel to argue that it does not "transfer" its citizens. Utilization of the power of expropriation, which is one of the strongest forces bestowed on a state, greatly sharpens the argument that Israel "transfers" its residents.[8]

The high court has allowed the expropriation of privately-owned Palestinian land for security purposes (such as building the separation barrier), and even for public purposes (such as building roads). However, the Supreme Court has never allowed the state to expropriate privately-owned, Palestinian land for the sole purpose of establishing an Israeli settlement. The expropriation of private land for the purpose of building settlements stands in stark contrast to the interpretation of international law adopted by the Israeli Supreme Court.

In the 1979 Elon Moreh case, the Supreme Court clarified that the building of settlements on privately-owned land, as compared with public land, is unlawful, subject to the "military needs" exception. The Court emphasized that "the principle of preserving an individual's property applies also under the laws of war that are expressed in section 46 of the Hague rules. A military rule that wishes to harm an individual's right to property must show a legal basis for it and cannot exempt itself from judicial review of its actions based on a claim of lack of justiciability."[9]

In an opinion piece written by a representative for Regavim, a think-tank which dedicates itself to researching land issues throughout Israel, a background to the law is given. "Property claims—often brought forward on behalf of Arabs by extremist anti-Israel NGOs—will need to be verified, since until now land not classified as state land in Judea and Samaria was automatically deemed private land regardless of its true status."[10] The Regavim claim that the Civil Administration charged with overseeing civilian life in Judea and Samaria, 1999, decided to reassess the state's earlier surveys and mappings of available state lands. A team of surveyors known as the State Property Delimitation Team, or the "Blue Line Team,"[11] was established to utilize technologies that earlier had been unavailable for the state's representative to review previous mapping. Since 1999 the "Blue Line Team" has been reevaluating the lines and redrawing their own blue lines in areas where even the slightest doubts arose. The consequences of this, according to Regavim, is that homes that previously was thought to be built, and standing on, state lands, with reassessments and new findings run the risk of having their homes demolished.

Many have questioned whether the legislation will survive judicial review by the Supreme Court. Israel's Attorney General Avichai Mandelblit has reportedly declared that if the law is challenged in court, he would not defend it against arguments that it violates the Fourth Geneva Convention. Mandelblit has argued that it is unconstitutional and states that the High Court, in a written brief, it was harmful and discriminatory toward the Palestinians. Accordingly, Justice Minister Ayelet Shaked hired private lawyer Harel Arnon to defend the law. Mandelblit's opposition is likely to help the petitioners swing the court.[12]

In a judgment rendered by Esther Hayut, the President of the High Court, the government, the Knesset, and the military commander for the West Bank were asked to explain why the Settlement Regulations Law should be "declared null and void, since it is unconstitutional."[13] She asked a larger group of defendants, including Mandelblit, the Civil Administration, and the Custodian of Abandoned Properties, to explain why it should be annulled and why it should be approved.

At issue is the fate of close to 4,000 illegal settler homes on private Palestinian property. Thirteen nongovernmental groups, including Peace Now, Yesh Din, and the Association for Civil Rights in Israel, petitioned the High Court against the law. Among the petitioners against the law is also Adalah whose lawyer Hassan Jabareen was quoted saying "that the government was trying to initiate a legal revolution."[14]

Mandelblit said the Settlements Regulations Law was too broad and blunt an instrument to use to carry out such transfers, which could only be done in limited cases where the principles of proportionality and reasonableness were fulfilled. The High Court has already frozen the law and few legal experts have predicted that the High Court will uphold the law, especially given Mandelblit's strong opposition. Despite this, the current government in Israel, with Justice Minister Ayelet Shaked has remained adamant that the law has a real shot with the High Court.[15]

NOTES

1. Tovah Lazaroff, Jeremy Bod Yonah, "Court: Israeli Government Must Defend Law Seizing Palestinian Property", *Jerusalem Post*, December 4 , 2017, http://www.jpost.com/Israel-News/High-Court-issues-interim-order-on-Settlements-Law-516970 (accessed June 10, 2018).

2. Israel, Ministry of Justice, "Regulation of Settlement in Judea and Samaria Law, 5777-2017," Law of Library of Congress. Global Research Center, "Israel: Law for the Regulation of Settlement in Judea and Samaria, 5777-2017," February 2017, Library of Congress, https://www.loc.gov/law/help/israel-settlement/judea-and-samaria.php (May 26, 2018). Scroll to issue no. 2604672, text of law archived at https://perma.cc/8ZKQ-3USL.

3. Israel, "Arrangement Law Passed in Second and Third Reading ," Knesset, http://main.knesset.gov.il/News/Press Releases/Pages/press6217g.aspx (in Hebrew; last accessed February 6, 2017), archived at https://perma.cc/ZKY8-3TWQ.

4. Israel, "Regulation of Settlement in Judea and Samaria Law, 5777-2017," §8.

5. Israel, "Regulation of Settlement in Judea and Samaria Law, 5777-2017," §9.

6. Israel, "Regulation of Settlement in Judea and Samaria Law, 5777-2017," §10.

7. Israel, Ministry of Justice, "Regulation of Settlement in Judea and Samaria Law 5777-2016," Knesset Draft Bills Issue No. 672, 44, explanatory notes for §§ 1 & 2 (December 7, 2016), http://knesset.gov.il/Laws/Data/BillKnesset/672/672.pdf (in Hebrew), archived as https://perma.cc/39G8-8XPG.

8. Israel, "Regulation of Settlement in Judea and Samaria Law, 5777-2017," Senior Foreign Law Specialist.

9. High Court of Justice. *'Izzat Muhammad Mustafa Duweikat et 16 al. v. 1. Government of Israel 2. Minister of Defense 3. Military Commander for the Judea and Samaria Area 4. Nablus District Military Commander 5. Felix Menahem 6. Shvut Avraham.* Case HCJ 390/79. September 6-October 22, 1979. http://www.hamoked.org/files/2010/1670_eng.pdf (accessed May 25, 2018).

10. Josh Hasten, "How the 'Blue Liners' forced the Regulation Law's passing," *Jerusalem Post,* February 13, 2017,https://www.jpost.com/Opinion/How-the-Blue-Liners-forced-the-Regulation-Laws-passing-481435(accessed June 10, 2018).

11. Josh Hasten, "How the 'Blue Liners' forced the Regulation Law's passing."

12. Jeremy Bod Yonah, "Court Hears Petitions Against Settlements Law; West Bank's Future In Balance", *Jerusalem Post*, June 3 , 2018, https://www.jpost.com/Arab-Israeli-Conflict/Court-hears-petitions-against-Settlements-Law-Future-West-Bank-in-balance-559024 (accessed June 10, 2018).

13. Tovah Lazaroff, Jeremy Bod Yonah, "Court: Israeli Government Must Defend Law Seizing Palestinian Property", *Jerusalem Post*, December 4 , 2017, http://www.jpost.com/Israel-News/High-Court-issues-interim-order-on-Settlements-Law-516970 (accessed June 10, 2018).

14. Jeremy Bod Yonah, "Court Hears Petitions Against Settlements Law; West Bank's Future In Balance", *Jerusalem Post*, June 3 , 2018, https://www.jpost.com/Arab-Israeli-Conflict/Court-hears-petitions-against-Settlements-Law-Future-West-Bank-in-balance-559024 (accessed June 10, 2018).

15. Yonah, "Court Hears Petitions Against Settlements Law."

Chapter Seven

Two Different Destinies, Two Separate Paths

The book's intention is to show nuances in a complex question. Few voices succeed better in this mission than Rabbi Menachem Froman and Shabtay Bendet. While Froman, in no uncertain terms, would be called "a hard core settler" or a "fanatic" by dogmatic voices in the west, his eternal love for, and of, the land would lead him to break taboos not even Israeli governments, US administrations and the European Union dared to. He would meet and talk to the founder and Hamas spiritual sheikh Ahmed Yassin. For peace and love he would be willing to do anything. He rejected the notion of expelling Jews from the West Bank and he was fully committed to live, and be governed, under a Palestinian state and governance. To Froman, living on the land was more essential, than who de facto was controlling it.

Shabtay Bendet life has been quite interesting as well. As a former Hasidic [ultra-orthodox Jew] he went from establishing illegal outposts [outposts not approved by the Israeli government] to fight for dismantling outposts he once was trying to establish. He is now active in Peace Now movement.

By sharing these stories, by giving a portrait of the thoughts from Froman and Bendet, it is my belief that behind their actions and active choices, lies a love so strong, so forceful and so indescribable for the Land and its People living there. Without understanding the love of the land, it is doubtful we will understand its people whether they are Arabs, Jews or Christians.

THE UNLIKELY PEACE ACTIVIST

Rabbi Menachem Froman, in an interview posted on January 31, 2015, said:

> One of my sons is called Tsuri Shalom. My strength is peace. So if religion is your devotion to God you are devoted to peace. Peace is the end of any human activity. Peace is the goal of our life. If we came here for religious reasons, you can also say that we came here to create peace, to work for peace. Every Jewish child is supposed to know the famous story of the non-Jew who came to one of our sages, Hillel is his name, and asked him to summarize the Torah, while he is standing on one leg, in one sentence.
>
> Hillel's answer was to quote the verse in Leviticus: Love your neighbor as you love yourself. The Palestinians are our neighbors. To love them and to be interested that they shall have what we have, freedom, Jerusalem (the beloved city as their as well as our capital).
>
> I remember me and another friend of mine. One of the mythological leaders of Gush Emunim. Uri Eli Tzur is his name, going in the night, in order to establish a settlement in Sebastia. This was few days after the birth of his firstborn son. And I asked him: Uri what do you want as a gift? And it was taken for granted that he will ask me for one of the Torah books. But he answered me: No I want a Hebrew Arab vocabulary. Because if we want to settle among the Arabs we have to understand them and we have to be able to talk to them.
>
> From my point of view, religion can be the bridge. The serious, genuine efforts of Israelis, Americans, Palestinians, Europeans to bring peace—all of those lack the power to take the power of religion seriously. And if they think about religion,

> they think religion is the reasons behind wars., not in contributing in peace. I cannot say that religion does not contribute to war, but one can, like nuclear power, also develop it for peace. In one of my many talks with Ahmad Yassin, the leader of Hamas, he defines the Oslo agreement. Our anti-religious powers and your anti-religious powers making an agreement to suppress religion. But I think it's part of evolution. You can make the nuclear energy an energy of peace.[1]

Rabbin Froman was one of the founders behind the settler movement Gush Emunim. Later he became the chief rabbi for Tekoa, a settlement in the heart of the West Bank. But he was also famous for his relationships with Palestinian leaders, including Sheikh Ahmed Yassin, the spiritual founder of Hamas. He was a settler and peace activist; deeply religious and a free-love advocate. He lived in the West Bank and preached an end to occupation. He was born in a secular family in Kfar Hasidim in northern Israel, studying in the prestigious Hebrew Reali School in Haifa before serving as a parachutist in the military and participating in the liberation of the Wailing Wall. After his military service, he found the religion. He participated in Mercaz HaRav and Yeshivat Hakotel and was inaugurated by renowned Rabbi Shlomo Goren and Avraham Shapira, both very influential in the thriving religious Zionist movement.

After his studies, he helped establish the Gush Emunim Movement, which was engaged in the settlement of the West Bank. He loved the biblical mountain landscape Gush Etzion, the settlement cluster outside Jerusalem, and lived there, first in Midgal Oz and later in Tekoa, which he helped to found. He studied Hassidic literature relentlessly, fascinated by the writings of Jewish mystics and their belief that love and joy were important parts of being faithful to God.

In an interview, Froman described how he considered it impossible to mend peace without taking into consideration the religious element. He tells the story of how Sheikh Ahmed Yassin once told him that he and Froman could bring peace in five minutes. Why?

Because both were believers. The interview with Froman goes on and the Haaretz reporter asks him: "You are trying to resolve the conflict between us and the Arabs, but there is also a split between a large part of the Israelis and settlers. What do you think about this?"[2]

Rabbi Froman answers: "There is a statement by [Andrei] Gromyko, who was Secretary of State of the Soviet Union. Peace is indivisible. My goal is not to create peace between us and the Palestinians. That is the result. Peace between a man and his fellow man, between a nation and its neighbor is all a kind of mental adjustment, a decision of the soul, which wants to move to the side of peace. It is necessary to purify the Jewish religion."[3]

Another interview with the same magazine describes Froman's philosophy.[4] Since the early 1980s, Froman devoted his life to peace, but his peace did not come from the left and did certainly not come from the right. Froman did not believe in nations—he believed in "the simple concept of neighbours acting with neighborly respect." Froman often stressed that it does not matter which nation actually rules the land as long as people go to school together or go to the same theater on Saturdays. Eventually, they will learn to get along and none of these distinctions will matter because we'll all peacefully co-exist.

He started calling for negotiations with Palestinians, heresy in the eyes of most rabbis in the occupied territories. He even started meeting with Palestinians leaders, though it was illegal at the time. He called on Israel to allow Palestinians to have their own country and their own national identity. He even said he does not mind living under Palestinian sovereignty, if needed. Over the years, his involvement with the peace movement deepened. He attended the Madrid Peace Conference in 1991 and developed a deep, meaningful relationship with the Arab-Israeli community as well. He even founded an Israeli-Palestinian peace organization, Eretz Shalom.

He was not a typical peace activist. The left was as confused about him as the right. He was a settler that supported negotiations and peace but also one who loathed the leftist dogma of evacuating the settlements as a necessary part of the peace process. He asked why anyone should be evicted from his home.

It is noteworthy that Froman remained to his last day a believer in the right of all Jews to live anywhere in Eretz Yisrael.[5] In July 1996 he wrote, "As a primitive religious Jew who is connected to the land that God gave my ancestors I can attest: This is also the reason that the connection between those who support Greater Israel (Eretz Yisrael ha-Shelamah) and the Palestinians has far greater potential [for success than the left]. This is because the Palestinians are also generally religious, or at least have a strong connection to their tradition, to their people, and to their land. What severs our connection is [only] hatred of the other."

One of his new solutions, which could be a form of "post-settler Zionism," was to distinguish between the state and the Jewish connection to the land. That is, to enable settlers to stay in their homes in the West Bank and become citizens of the State of Palestine. Froman understood the contradiction between hating the other and loving the land as such. Froman believed in the power of religion to repair gaps and bridge cultures. The Israeli-Palestinian conflict was for him religious in nature, so it was up to religious figures—not politicians—to solve it.

Froman understood that hatred is temporary but love is eternal. To find humanity even in its bitterest enemies.

THE FORMER SETTLER THAT SUDDENLY STARTED WORKING AGAINST EVERYTHING HE WAS TAUGHT TO BELIEVE IN

Shabtay Bendet was one of the founders of Rehelim—the West Bank's first illegal outpost[6] —who facilitated the covert transport of trailers to the hilltop community south of Nablus in the dead of night. But these days, instead of trying to outfox Israel Defense Forces soldiers on the hilltops of the West Bank, he is fighting the Civil Administration bureaucrats who have ruled in favor of further normalizing Rehelim, along with other wildcat communities the government has sought to legalize. "You can't ignore the humor of it all," Bendet said, smirking slightly as he reflected on the moment two months later. "I know what I did in the past, and I knew it would catch up with me at some point." In an interview with the *Times of Israel*, Bendet said he was aware of the many ironies that come with his transformation from hard-core settler to left-wing activist.

Bendet's spent his childhood in a religious home in Tel Aviv. He was active in the religious Zionist Bnei Akiva youth movement and studied in Jerusalem's Machon Meir yeshiva after graduating high school. After a year at Machon Meir, Bendet enlisted in the army and served as a commander in the Givati infantry brigade. Following his discharge, he moved to the northern town of Safed to continue his Torah studies at a yeshiva. He married and had children. As he became more religious, he and his wife looked for opportunities to move to the West Bank.

The story of Rehelim began in October 1991, when a bus of right-wing activists, heading from the Shiloh settlement to a Tel Aviv protest against the upcoming Madrid Peace Conference, came under fire from a group of Palestinian terrorists. The attack killed Rachel Drouk, a mother of seven from Shiloh. Immediately after burying their friend, a group of twenty-five women made their way to the hilltop where she was murdered, marking it as the next spot for a Jewish settlement.

While the army initially resisted the requests of the women to remain on the hilltop, Israeli authorities eventually acquiesced and allowed them to stay for the duration of the seven-day *shiva* mourning period.

When the week ended, a deal was struck with the army allowing the women to erect a number of makeshift tents, which would be guarded by a new military outpost. There were no permanent buildings, but settlers were allowed to visit freely and to periodically stay the night.

Rehelim, which is the Hebrew plural of "Rachel," is also named for Rachel Weiss, who was burned to death along with her three children in a Molotov cocktail attack on a bus outside Jericho in 1988, and for Rachel the biblical matriarch.

The radicalizing yeshiva student Shabtay Bendet moved from Safed to the hilltop along with his wife and their eight-month-old daughter. "I felt like I was doing something meaningful. I didn't want to move to a community that already existed. Our central trigger was to create something that could not be undone." Upon arrival in Rehelim, Bendet found agricultural work in the hilltop community of Shvut Rachel, "where the goal was to expand settlement to as much land as possible under the guise of agriculture." For Times of Israel Bendet says that the settlers saw Palestinians as an enemy. "The army was there to protect us, and we had a good relationship with them overall, but we also factored how that relationship could be manipulated to our benefit."[7]

In a pattern that would recur throughout the West Bank in the years since, Bendet said the government grudgingly accepted Rehelim's existence after the fact, but only to an extent. The settlers were forced to play a cat-and-mouse game with the Israeli soldiers who protected them, trying to catch the 18- to 21-year-olds off guard long enough to install additional caravans on the hilltop.

Bendet also studied at the radical Od Yosef Chai Yeshiva, which at the time was located at the Joseph's Tomb shrine site in the heart of the Palestinian city of Nablus. He grew very close to the yeshiva's president, the far-right Hasidic rabbi Yitzhak Ginsburgh. Bendet became "a Chabadnik."

But his soul-searching continued, and he went through further personal transformations as he searched for what he called being his "proper place." "I had thought that if I were to become more and more hardcore, I would find happiness and that the disquiet would cease," he said. "But after years of that not happening, I began wondering if this [ultra-Orthodox lifestyle] isn't the truth and that maybe it's wrong to take an extreme view on everything, as if it's all black and white."[8]

A formative experience in his decision to veer leftward was the 2005 evacuation of the settlement of Homesh. "People say that the feeling during these evacuations is like an organ being ripped out of your body and that it's even worse because it's your own brothers doing it," Bendet explained. "I felt this at Homesh as well, but there was also a part of me that thought, 'Maybe there's more to this. Maybe we're exaggerating by thinking that everything related to these communities is the most important thing in the world.'"[9]

Eventually Bendet decided that he was no longer religious. Bendet remained in Rehelim with his family for another three years, but stopped covered his head or keeping Shabbat. "People probably thought, 'Oh, that's just Shabtay,' but my journey really did not have that many steps. I was religious, then I became Haredi, and now I am secular. That's it."[10]

In 2009, after twelve years in Rehelim, Bendet, his wife, and their entourage of children, which by then had swelled to six, moved to the central city of Modiin. Acting on his desire to better understand the conflict by meeting the other side, the ex-settler became a West Bank correspondent for the Galey Israel radio station and later for the Walla news site.

"I used the opportunity to meet with Palestinians as much as I could," he said. "I would cover every protest, embedding myself within their population in an attempt to truly understand where they are coming from." As a news reporter Bendet saw his views slowly move further to the left with each year on the job. "As journalist I began learning how discriminatory building regulations are against Palestinians." Regardless, Bendet said he was "fanatic" about keeping his political views out of his work. "I wanted to be able to observe from above, rather than be part of the story," he said.[11]

His views were further challenged in Amona, an outpost that was evacuated in February 2017. Bendet was at the outpost as a member of the press, but while he was not an active player in the demolition, his eldest son was.

Bendet said, "we talked about it before, and I knew he would be there. After all, I had educated him for this sort of thing."[12]

From a young age, Bendet had taught his children about the importance of the settlement movement, and he said it was "only natural" for his son to be among the hundreds of youths who descended on Amona last February to protest the evacuation. "I can't suddenly get up and say everything I taught him was nonsense," he said. "I try to give him a different point of view when possible, but I understood why he was there." It was definitely difficult to see, but I composed myself and asked one of the soldiers there if I could try to convince him to leave of his own volition," Bendet recalled. "I told him that he fought, protested and did his part, but that it was time to go." When the teenager refused, he was hoisted up by four soldiers and lugged out of the home, crying as Bendet walking behind him, carrying his son's bag. "It wasn't easy, but it is what it is" he's quoted saying. In September 2017 Bendet joined the Peace Now movement.[13]

NOTES

1. Menachem Froman, "Rabbi Menachem Froman, Settler, Peach Advocate," interview, posted by Peter Cohn, *Vimeo*, January 31, 2015, https://vimeo.com/118344294 (accessed May 25, 2018).

2. Ayelett Shani, "West Bank's Rabbi Menachem Froman Has the Solution to the Conflict," *Haaretz*, July 20, 2012, http://www.haaretz.com/israel-news/the-west-bank-s-rabbi-menachem-froman-has-the-solution-to-the-conflict-1.452325 (accessed May 27, 2018)

3. Shani, "West Bank's Rabbi Menachem Froman Has the Solution to the Conflict."

4. Asher Schechter, "Rebbe With a Cause: The Unconventional Truths of Menachem Froman," *Haaretz*, March 6, 2013, http://www.haaretz.com/israel-news/rebbe-with-a-cause-the-unconventional-truths-of-menachem-froman.premium-1.507710 (accessed May 27, 2018).

5. Shaul Magid, "West Bank Rabbi Menachem Froman's Zionist Post-Zionism, and What It Can Teach American Jews," August 4, 2016, *Tablet Magazine*, http://www.tabletmag.com/jewish-news-and-politics/192626/froman-zionist-post-zionism (accessed May 26, 2018).

6. Former settler is bent on dismantling outposts he once toiled to establish; see Jacob Magid, "A Former Settler is Bent on Dismantling Outposts He Once Toiled to Establish," *Times of Israel*, January 12, 2018, https://www.timesofisrael.com/why-shabtay-bendet-is-working-to-dismantle-settlements-he-toiled-to-establish/ (accessed May 26, 2018).

7. Magid, "Former Settler."

8. Magid, "Former Settler."

9. Magid, "Former Settler."

10. Magid, "Former Settler."

11. Magid, "Former Settler."

12. Magid, "Former Settler."

13. Magid, "Former Settler."

Conclusions

Isidor Isaac Rabi, the Nobel laureate in physics was once asked, "Why did you become a scientist, rather than a doctor or lawyer or businessman, like the other immigrant kids in your neighborhood?"

Dr. Rabi's answer: "My mother made me a scientist without ever intending it. Every other Jewish mother in Brooklyn would ask her child after school: 'So? Did you learn anything today?' But not my mother. She always asked me a different question. 'Izzy,' she would say, 'did you ask a good question today?' That difference—asking good questions—made me become a scientist!"[1]

What separates good books from ordinary books is its ability to raise questions.

If one accepts the premise that Israel is occupying some areas and as an occupying force is forbidden to change laws from previous sovereigns, it becomes relevant which are the laws and as such, how are they followed? My aim with this book was to look at this angle with regard to Israeli settlements and to go deeper to understand the rationale behind land policies.

The book is not necessarily a full rejection of the arguments that have been advocated by different scholars that seek to brand Israel's settlement enterprise as illegal, nor is it to be understood as a full acceptance of those arguments at hand. Rather, I want this book to point out the nuances in an infective question. The idea is not to take sides on who is right or wrong, but rather to give the reader an insight into the arguments made by Israel and its judiciary that have not been properly addressed nor researched by earlier scholars.

How did I become intrigued with the question of Israeli Land Politics beyond the Geneva Convention? The answer to that question can only be properly understood and explained by several factors. The first factor has to do with the fact that presence of Jews in West Bank has been a continuous feature since time immemorial. Surely one can cast a doubt, or contest, the numbers of Jews in the West Bank since time of immemorial, and that its numbers and figures has fluctuated dependent on how difficult the persecution against the Jewish people has been. One can also completely reject the notion that Jews are being part of the Israeli people and identity (a notion commonly used in the Arab world as a strategy for negating Jewish connection to the land and region itself) and, instead view inhabitants of the West Bank exclusively as Palestinians. In the so called "Palestine Papers"[2] the Palestinian Negotiating Team discusses options for dealing with property claims of Jews within the West Bank acquired before the beginning of the occupation, covering Ottoman and British periods, Jordanian Rule of the West Bank and Egyptian rule of Gaza. The right also extends to the descendants of such Jews. So even the Palestinians admit Jewish presence in the West Bank prior 1967.

Regardless of how one view oneself and others, individuals' adherent to Jewish belief system, *have been* a continuous feature in the West Bank since time immemorial.

The Israeli politician Arie Eliav suggested that after peace with Arab agreement, Jewish settlement east and west of Jordan could be possible but those Jews would have to be citizens in the State of Palestine,[3] the mirror image of the Arabs in Israel that are citizens. This is a further verification that the settlement ethos had an impact of both left and right-wing Jews, as well as between secular and religious Jews.

The second factor behind my interest of examine Israeli Land politics had to do with the inability, negligence, and refusal to understand the context, and grounding statements, behind the paragraphs and articles that are most cited in regard to Israeli settlements. Israel is often accused of changing borders in violation of international law. That statement needs to be problematized.

International law is a European concept that was created to cement the European colonial era, to freeze the world in 1960 era boundaries and to freeze it in the conditions Europe created. We still live under the shadow of Eurocentric laws and attempts to impose these views on the world. International law is still predicted on denying indigenous people all over the world the say in their own destiny, by saying borders and rules made by colonial – governments are the only way to do things. To understand the context in which international law and norms are formed is also essential when judging actors' behaviour. The settlement issue is highlighted foremost through Convention (IV) relative to the Protection of Civilian Persons in Time of War, Article 49.[4]

The authoritative interpretation of the International Committee of the Red Cross (IRCC), the body entrusted with the implementation of the Fourth Geneva Convention, in which the purpose of Article 49 is stated as follows: "It is intended to prevent a practice adopted during the Second World War by certain Powers, which transferred portions of their own population to occupied territory for political and racial reasons or in order, as they claimed, to colonize those territories. Such transfers worsened the economic situation of the native population and endangered their separate existence as a race."[5] Not only the failure to disregard and understand continuous Jewish presence and history since time immemorial, by invoking a paragraph that in its commentaries make a resemblance to Nazi practice, it is also a highly problematic usage.

First it can be interpreted as a way of associating Israeli Land policies as equivalent of those from being materialized in the Nazi regime. Second of all, which I will address more thoroughly below, is that Article 49 remains only to be used in reference to Israeli policies and in no other cases of occupations.

Regardless of whether one endorse the narrative of the Palestinians or the Israelis, there is this constant question hanging in the air: Which laws are to be upheld? The reasoning surrounding the concept of an occupation rests on the assumption that the occupier is in power instead of someone else. As an occupier you are forced to uphold laws (unless it is absolute necessary to change them) from previous administrations. This aspect in the Israeli-Palestinian settlement issue has not been thoroughly addressed and it is a vital component in the sphere of Israeli land politics.

On December 23, 2016, Barack Obama did what President Jimmy Carter had done before him in Security Resolutions 446, 452, and 465 from 1979-1980. These were all resolutions against Israeli settlements.

On the surface it appeared to be, in reference to earlier UN positions, a quite reasonable resolution.

One of the major differences from the previous resolutions adopted was that time, dynamics, and above all, politics have changed the environment. In the 1970s, and early 1980s during the Carter administration, there was no mutual recognition between Palestine Liberation Organization (PLO) and Israel. There was no Oslo Treaty Interim Agreement, which divides the West Bank into A, B, and C areas. The resolution gave rise to more questions than it appeared to give answers.

If Israel has committed the crime of allowing its citizens to live in what is defined as occupied, or disputed, reasonably it should apply to every Israeli citizen who has moved to the disputed areas, not only to Jews. This would include thousands of Bedouin and

Israeli Arabs who moved into eastern Jerusalem neighborhoods, such as Jebel Mukaber, Bet Sahour, Bet Safafa, Beit Hanina, and Shuafat, and who built tens of thousands of illegal homes and businesses. And, what about Arabs who moved from areas controlled by the Palestine National Authority (PNA) and those from Arab countries who moved into Area C? Are they also criminals?

That nuance is required when referring to the illegality of *all* Jewish settlements, is evident in the Elon Moreh verdict. In that verdict the Israeli Supreme Court stated that from a pure security aspect, it cannot be doubted that the presence in the territories of settlements- even "civilian" settlements- of citizens of the occupying power contributes appreciably to security in that territory and makes it easier for the army to carry out its task. "One does not have to be a military and security expert to realize that terrorist elements operate more easily in an area inhabited only by a population that is indifferent or is sympathetic towards the enemy than in an area where there are also persons likely to look out for them and to report any suspicious movement to the authorities."[6]

The failure to: (a) acknowledge the division of areas and responsibilities between the Palestinian Authority and Israel that the Oslo agreement accomplished; (b) of realizing that not all settlements, as long as they have military purposes, can be considered illegal, was highly problematic since it completely neglected requisitions in kind and services for the needs of the army of occupation.[7] The United Nation Security Council's Resolution 2334 was a practical, concrete example of the complexities at hand when viewing settlements in a context of black and white dimensions.

What about ownership issues? As mentioned, many of Middle Eastern countries have been shaped by the Ottoman institution of state ownership of land which is rooted in Islamic religious law. Israel is no exception. What if Israel and the Palestinians like most of Western world would adopt the policies of private land ownership? The Israeli journalist Orit Arfa might be on to something when she foresees a situation where it breaks both sides out of the harmful, irrational, and hopeless "Jewish versus Arab land" continuum. With individuals owning land, disputes would be taken out of the nationalistic sphere and off the international stage. They would be settled privately—not between nations—in lower, local courts, as in the rest of the world.

An additional aspect that generates questions is expressed through the principle of the sovereign equality of states which finds expression in Article 2, paragraph 1, of the 1945 *Charter of the United Nations.*[8] It has been described by the International Court of Justice as one of the fundamental principles of the international legal order. Respect for sovereign equality requires not only uniformity in the statement of rules, but also uniformity in the application of rules. By expressing the opinion that *all Israeli settlements infringe international law* there is reason to believe that the United Nations Security Council, through its resolutions against Israeli settlements, holds Israel to a different standard in relation to other territories that qualify as occupied under international law, such as Russia/Crimea, Morocco/Western Sahara, and Turkey/Northern Cyprus. Israel has the right to be treated in the same way as other states, and therefore care needs to be taken to formulate, as objectively as possible, the rules and principles of international law, and also to apply them in a uniform fashion, rather than adopting and applying rules and interpretations solely in relation to Israel and Palestine.

As showed by a 2016 article from Professor Eugene Kantorovich and and Penny Grunseid, the United Nations uses an entirely different rhetoric and set of legal concepts when dealing with Israel compared with situations of occupation or settlements world-wide.[9] For example, Israel is referred to as the "Occupying Power" 530 times in General Assembly resolutions. Yet in seven major instances of past or present prolonged military occupation—Indonesia in East Timor, Turkey in northern Cyprus, Russia in areas of

Georgia, Morocco in Western Sahara, Vietnam in Cambodia, Armenia in areas of Azerbaijan, and Russia in Ukraine's Crimea—the number is *zero*. The United Nations has not called any of these countries an "Occupying Power." Not even once.

Most striking are the resolutions refer to Article 49, paragraph 6, which states that the "Occupying Power shall not deport or transfer parts of its own civilian population into the territory it occupies." This is the provision that the entire legal case against Israel settlements is based upon. Yet no U.N. body has ever invoked Article 49, paragraph 6, in relation to any of the occupations mentioned above.

In this book, I discussed two visionaries that represent different spectrums. Menachem Froman was the hard-core settler who lived in the West Bank. But he was also famous for relationships with Palestinian leaders, including Sheikh Ahmed Yassin, the spiritual founder of Hamas. He was a settler and peace activist; he was deeply religious and a free-love advocate. He lived in the West Bank and preached an end to occupation. He tells the story of how Sheikh Ahmed Yassin once told him that he and Froman could bring peace in five minutes. Why? Because both were believers.

The other voice I wanted to bring into this equation is Shabtay Bendet. He was one of the founders of Rehelim—the West Bank's first illegal outpost. His message in the interview he gave to the *Times of Israel* "*it's wrong to take an extreme view on everything, as if it's all black and white*"[10] and this concept is what I have tried to conveyed.

Whether Israel deviates or complies with the Ottoman Land Law and the amendments made by the British, might be a subject of interest for future research. My aim of writing this book is to shed nuances in land expropriation. The laws enacted to deal with these matters was typical of its era and of its colonial settings. To quote the District Court's ruling in Beersheba, one of the more important cases in terms of land acquisition:

> The harsh nature of the provisions of the Acquisition Law and the non-use of the expropriation of land arrangements prescribed in the Land Ordinance, can only be understood from the aspect of the special historical circumstances of the early days of the State; against the background of the needs of the time and when lands were abandoned by their owners as a result of the events of the war.[11]

I began my closing remarks by a quotation from Isidor I. Rabi and this is how I want my book to be read and understood.

NOTES

1. Isidor Isaac Rabi, quoted in Letter to the Editor, by Donald Sheff, "Issy, Did You Ask a Good Question Today?" *New York Times*, January 19, 1988, A26, https://mobile.nytimes.com/1988/01/19/opinion/l-izzy-did-you-ask-a-good-question-today-712388.html (accessed June 4, 2018).
2. Al Jazeera, "The Palestine Papers NSU Draft Memo Re: Rights of Jews Within the OPT Acquired pre-1967," September 2008, http://www.ajtransparency.com/en/projects/thepalestinepapers/201218203525218283.html (accessed May 24, 2018).
3. Gershom Gorenberg, *The Accidental Empire: Israel and the Birth of the Settlements, 1967–1977* (New York: Holt Paperbacks; 2007), 176.
4. ICRC, "Convention (IV) Relative to the Protection of Civilian Persons in Time of War," Article 49, https://ihl-databases.icrc.org/ihl/COM/380-600056?OpenDocument (accessed July 3 2018).
5. Israel, "Levy Commission Report."
6. High Court of Justice. *'Izzat Muhammad Mustafa Duweikat et 16 al. v. 1. Government of Israel 2. Minister of Defense 3. Military Commander for the Judea and Samaria Area 4. Nablus District Military Commander 5. Felix Menahem 6. Shvut Avraham.* Case HCJ 390/79. September 6-October 22, 1979. http://www.hamoked.org/files/2010/1670_eng.pdf (accessed May 25, 2018).
7. Convention (IV) respecting the Laws and Customs of War on Land and its Annex, Article 52, (accessed July 3 2018).
8. United Nations, *Charter of the United Nations*, June 26, 1945, http://www.un.org/en/charter-united-nations/index.html (accessed May 25, 2018).
9. Eugene Kontorovich and Penny Grunseid, "At the U.N., Only Israel Is an 'Occupying Power,'" *Wall Street Journal*, September 13, 2016, https://

www.wsj.com/articles/at-the-u-n-only-israel-is-an-occupying-power-1473808544 (accessed May 26, 2018).

10. Jacob Magid, "A Former Settler is Bent on Dismantling Outposts He Once Toiled to Establish." *Times of Israel*, January 12, 2018. https://www.timesofisrael.com/why-shabtay-bendet-is-working-to-dismantle-settlements-he-toiled-to-establish/ (accessed May 26, 2018); emphasis mine.

11. The District Court in Beersheba Civil Case File Nos. 7161/06, 7275/06, 7276/06 1114/07, 1115/07, 5278/08, El Uqbi vs The State of Israel. District Court Judgement of March 15, 2012.

Glossary

BADIL. Resource Center for Palestinian Residency and Refugees Rights.

Beit El. In the *Beit El* case of 1978 the Israeli High Court approved civilian settlement for reasons of general security. The state declared that the right of the settlers to remain in Beit El would expire upon the termination of its military necessity.

B'Tselem. The Israeli Information Center for Human Rights in the Occupied Territories.

COHRE. The Centre on Housing Rights and Evictions .

Elon Moreh verdict. Israel Supreme Court decided 1979 that civilian settlements that does not meet military requirements is contravened international law.

Geneva Conventions. Comprise four treaties, and three additionalprotocols, that establish the standards of international law for humanitarian treatment in war.

The Hague Convention. Series of international treaties and declarations.

JNF. Jewish National Fund.

Judea and Samaria. The biblical term of the West Bank.

Kushan. Ottoman land deed.

Land Ordinance of 1943. Acquisition for Public Purposes.

Land Ordinance 1928. Investigating the transfer of rights according to specific procedures until it reaches back to the allocation's source.

Mahlul. Abandoned land.

Matruka. Lands held in common for use either of the public (such as roads, rivers) or of a village or a group of communities for grazing or woodcutting.

Mevkufe. Lands possessed in mortmain, but tenanted by a kind of copyhold.

Miri. Property over which the right of occupation or of tenure can be enjoyed by a private person, provided that such right has been granted by the State. The absolute ownership remains vested in the Government, but the grant is in perpetuity, subject to certain conditions.

Mewat. Dead and undeveloped land.

Muajele. Immediate payment given in exchange for the right to possess and is collected by the official for the Government.

Mulk. Private or freehold land.

Ottoman Land Code. The central piece of legislation on landed property in the nineteenth century.

Planning and Building Law. Authorizes local planning commissions to issue expropriation orders.

Tapu. Legal document establishing the absolute ownership right to the acquired property

Tasarruf. Person in possession.

Waqf. Habous or mortmain property, is an inalienable charitable endowment under Islamic law.

Bibliography

ABC News. "Clinton Denies Bush Agreement With Israel on Settlement." *ABC News* (blog), June 14, 2009. http://blogs.abcnews.com/george/2009/06/clinton-denies-bush-agreement-with-israel-on-settlements.html.

Abrams, Elliott. "Hillary Is Wrong About the Settlements." *Wall Street Journal*, June 26, 2009. https://www.wsj.com/articles/SB124588743827950599 (accessed May 24, 2018).

Adler, Gerald M. "West Bank: A Response." *Journal* (Scotland), September 14, 2009. http://www.journalonline.co.uk/Magazine/54-9/1006961.aspx (accessed May 24, 2018).

Ahren, Raphael, and *TOI* Staff. "Israel Will Curb Settlement Expansion to Satisfy Trump." *Times of Israel*, March 31, 2017. https://www.timesofisrael.com/israel-says-it-will-curb-settlement-expansion-to-satisfy-trump/ (accessed May 24, 2018).

Al Jazeera. "The Palestine Papers: NSU Draft Memo Re: Rights of Jews Within the OPT Acquired pre-1967." September 2008. http://www.ajtransparency.com/en/projects/thepalestinepapers/201218203525218283.html (accessed May 24, 2018).

American President Project. "Interview with the President Jimmy Carter, Question-and-Answer Session With Foreign Correspondents." April 12, 1980. http://www.presidency.ucsb.edu/ws/?pid=33269 (accessed May 24, 2018).

———. "George Bush, The President's News Conference Following Discussions With Prime Minister Toshiki Kaifu of Japan in Palm Springs, California." March 3, 1990. http://www.presidency.ucsb.edu/ws/?pid=18215 (accessed May 24, 2018).

Arfa, Onit. "Who REALLY owns the Land of Israel?" *Jewish Journal*, December 31, 2013. http://jewishjournal.com/opinion/marty_kaplan/125677/who-really-owns-the-land-of-israel/ (accessed May 24, 2018).

Avner, Yehuda. *The Prime Ministers: An Intimate Narrative of Israeli Leadership*. New Milford, CT: Toby Press, 2010.

BADIL Staff. "Land Ownership in Palestine/Israel (1920-2000)." *Stocktaking and Perspectives* 5 (Spring 2002). http://www.badil.org/en/component/k2/item/1055-land-ownership-in-palestine.html (accessed May 25, 2018).

Beaumont, Peter. "Were Other Trump Aides Lobbying for Israel Illicitly Alongside Michael Flynn?" *Guardian*, December 1, 2017. https://www.theguardian.com/us-news/2017/dec/01/michael-flynn-israel-lobbying-russia-united-nations (accessed May 25, 2018).

Belman, Ted. "Are the Territories Disputed or Not?" (updated). *Israpundit* (blog). October 3, 2010. http://www.israpundit.org/28440/ (accessed May 25, 2018).

Bedein, David. "President Ford´s Legacy for Israel." *Behind: Israel Resource Review*. January 2, 2007. http://israelbehindthenews.com/president-fords-legacy-for-israel/5187 (accessed May 25, 2018).

Ben Ami, Shlomo. *Scars of War, Wounds of Peace: The Israeli-Arab Tragedy*. Oxford: Oxford University Press, 2007.

Benvenisti, Eyal. *The International Law of Occupation*. New ed. Princeton, NJ: Princeton University Press, 2004.

Blum, Yehuda Zvi. *The Missing Reversioner: Reflections on the Status of Judea and Samaria*. Jerusalem: Israel Law Review Association, under the auspices of The Faculty of Law, Hebrew University of Jerusalem, 1968. First published in *Israel Law Review* 3, no. 2 (April 1968): 279-301.

Briggs, Ari. "Beware Ottoman Land Law!" *Jerusalem Post*, July 30, 2015. http://www.jpost.com/Opinion/Beware-Ottoman-land-law-410708 (accessed May 31, 2018).

B'Tselem, "Under the Guise of Legality: Israel's Declarations of State Land in the West Bank." Report. February 2012. https://www.btselem.org/download/201203_under_the_guise_of_legality_eng.pdf (accessed May 25, 2018).

Bunton, Martin. "Demarcating the British Colonial State: Land Settlement in the Palestine *Jiftlik* Villages of Sajad and Qazaza." In *New Perspectives on Property and Land in the Middle East*, edited by Roger Owen, 121–59 .Cambridge, MA: Center for Middle Eastern Studies, Harvard University Press, 2000.

Centre on Housing Rights and Evictions (CHOHRE), and BADIL Resource Center for Palestinian Residency and Refugees Rights. "Ruling Palestine: A History of the Legally Sanctioned Jewish-Israeli Seizure of Land and Housing in Palestine." May 2005. http://www.badil.org/phocadownloadpap/Badil_docs/publications/Ruling%20Palestine.pdf (accessed May 25, 2018).

Chicago Tribune. "Bush Speech Excerpts." *Chicago Tribune*, April 5, 2002. http://articles.chicagotribune.com/2002-04-05/news/0204050329_1_responsible-palestinian-leaders-palestinian-authority-middle-east (accessed May 25, 2018).

Clinton, Bill, and George W. Bush. "U.S. Presidential Statements on Settlements." *Washington Post*, January 7, 2001 and April 4, 2002. Posted online

May 23, 2009. http://www.washingtonpost.com/wp-dyn/content/article/2009/05/23/AR2009052301871_2.html (accessed May 27, 2018).

Council of the League of Nations. "The Palestine Mandate." London. July 24, 1922. http://avalon.law.yale.edu/20th_century/palmanda.asp (accessed May 29, 2018).

Efrat, Elisha. *Geography and Politics in Israel since 1967*. New York: Routledge, 2005.

Forman, Geremy. "A Tale of Two Regions: Diffusion of the Israeli '50 Percent Rule' from the Galilee to the Occupied West Bank." *Law & Social Inquiry* 34, no 3 (Summer 2009): 671–711.

Friedman, Thomas L. "Baker Cites Israel For Settlements." *New York Times*, May 23, 1991, A5. http://www.nytimes.com/1991/05/23/world/baker-cites-israel-for-settlements.html (accessed May 25, 2018).

Froman, Menachem. "Rabbi Menachem Froman, Settler, Peach Advocate." Interview, posted by Peter Cohn. *Vimeo*. January 31, 2015. https://vimeo.com/118344294 (accessed May 25, 2018).

Gorenberg, Gershom. *The Accidental Empire: Israel and the Birth of the Settlements, 1967-1977* . New York: Holt Paperbacks; 2007.

Gross, Aeyal M. *The Writing On the Wall: Rethinking the International Law of Occupation*. Cambridge: Cambridge University Press, 2017.

Gwertzman, Bernard. "State Department; About the "West Bank and the Emperor's Clothes." *New York Times*, August 25, 1983, D2. http://www.nytimes.com/1983/08/25/us/state-department-about-the-west-bank-and-the-emperor-s-clothes.html (accessed May 25, 2018).

The Hague Initiative for International Cooperation (thinc). "The Hague Statement of Jurists on the Israel-Palestine Conflict." Discussion paper. 2017. http://www.thinc.info/wp-content/uploads/2017/11/The-Hague-Statement_20171031.pdf (accessed May 25, 2018).

Haklai, Oded, and Neophytos Loizedes, eds. *Settlers In Contested Lands: Territorial Disputes and Ethnic Conflict*. Stanford, CA: Stanford University Press, 2015.

Hoffman, Carl. "Who Owns the Holy City? The Jerusalem Question." *Jerusalem Post*, May 13, 2017. http://www.jpost.com/In-Jerusalem/Who-owns-the-Holy-City-484366 (accessed May 25, 2018).

Holzman-Gazit, Yifat. *Land Expropriation in Israel: Law Culture and Society*. Aldershot, UK: Ashgate, 2007. Reprint. New York: Routledge, 2016.

Ignatius, David. "Obama on Israeli Settlements." *Washington Post*, June 4, 2009. http://www.washingtonpost.com/wp-dyn/content/article/2009/06/03/AR2009060303241.html (accessed May 25, 2018).

International Committee of the Red Cross (ICRC). "Convention (IV) Relative to the Protection of Civilian Persons in Time of War." Geneva. August 12, 1949. ihl-databases.icrc.org/applic/ihl/ihl.nsf/Treaty.xsp?action=openDocument&documentId=AE2D398352C5B028C12563CD002D6B5C (accessed May 25, 2018).

———. "Convention (IV) Respecting the Laws and Customs of War on Land and Its Annex: Regulations Concerning the Laws and Customs of War on Land. Annex to the Convention: Article 43. Section 3. Military Authority Over the Territory of the Hostile State." The Hague. October 18, 1907. https://ihl-databases.icrc.org/ihl/WebART/195-200053? (accessed May 25, 2018).

———. "Practice Relating to Rule 103, Collective Punishments," https://ihl-databases.icrc.org/customary-ihl/eng/docs/v2_rul_rule103 (accessed June 2, 2018).

———. "Occupation and International Humanitarian Law: Questions and Answers." August 8, 2004. https://www.icrc.org/eng/resources/documents/misc/634kfc.htm (accessed May 25, 2018).

Israel. *Al-Uqbi et al. v. State of Israel*. Case [C.A.] 4220/12. Supreme Court Judgement of May 14, 2015.

———. "Arrangement Law Passed in Second and Third Reading." Knesset. http://main.knesset.gov.il/News/Press Releases/Pages/press6217g.aspx (in Hebrew; last accessed February 6, 2017), archived at https://perma.cc/ZKY8-3TWQ.

———. *Ayyub v. Minister of Defense*. (1978) 33 (2) P. D 113 (*Beth El* case). English summary: 9 Israel Yearbook on Human Rights (1979) 337.

———. High Court of Justice. *Duweikat et al. v. Government of Israel et al.* Judgment. HCJ 390/79. October 22, 1979. See http://www.hamoked.org/Document.aspx?dID=1670 (accessed May 25, 2018).

———. High Court of Justice. *'Izzat Muhammad Mustafa Duweikat et 16 al. v. 1. Government of Israel 2. Minister of Defense 3. Military Commander for the Judea and Samaria Area 4. Nablus District Military Commander 5. Felix Menahem 6. Shvut Avraham.* Case HCJ 390/79. September 6-October 22, 1979. http://www.hamoked.org/files/2010/1670_eng.pdf (accessed May 25, 2018).

———. "The Levy Commission Report on the Legal Status of Building in Judea and Samaria." Translated by Regavim (2014). June 21, 2012. http://www.regavim.org/levy-report-translated-into-english/ (accessed May 26, 2018).

———. Ministry of Foreign Affairs. "Address by PM Ariel Sharon at the Fourth Herzliya Conference." December 18, 2003. www.mfa.gov.il/mfa/pressroom/2003/pages/address%20by%20pm%20ariel%20sharon%20at%20the%20fourth%20herzliya.aspx (accessed May 26, 2018).

———. Ministry of Foreign Affairs. "The Judiciary: The Court System." 2013. www.mfa.gov.il/mfa/aboutisrael/state/democracy/pages/the%20judiciary-%20the%20court%20system.aspx (accessed May 26, 2018).

———. Israel Ministry of Foreign Affairs, "Israeli Settlements and International Law," November 2015, www.mfa.gov.il/mfa/foreignpolicy/peace/guide/pages/israeli%20settlements%20and%20international%20law.aspx, (accessed July 2, 2018).

———. Ministry of Justice. "Regulation of Settlement in Judea and Samaria Law, 5777, 2017." Law of Library of Congress. Global Research Center.

"Israel: Law for the Regulation of Settlement in Judea and Samaria, 5777–2017." February 2017. Library of Congress. https://www.loc.gov/law/help/israel-settlement/judea-and-samaria.php (May 26, 2018).

———. Ministry of Justice. "Regulation of Settlement in Judea and Samaria Law 5777-2016." December 7, 2016. http://knesset.gov.il/Laws/Data/Bill-Knesset/672/672.pdf (in Hebrew), archived as https://perma.cc/39G8-8XPG.

———. Office of the Deputy Attorney General (International Law). "International Agreements and International Litigation." Civil Case File Nos. 716/06, 7275/06,7276/06, 1114/07,1115/07, 5278/08. http://www.justice.gov.il/En/Units/HumanRightsAndForeignRelations/Pages/default.aspx (accessed May 26, 2018).

———. State Property Delimitation Team. http://www.law.idf.il/163-6731-en/Patzar.aspx?SearchText=state land

Jewish Agency. "Historical Aliyah." December 18, 2005. http://www.jewishagency.org/historical-aliyah/content/23440 (accessed July 2, 2018).

———. "Modern Zionist Aliyot to Israel About the waves of Jewish immigration to Israel (Aliot) 1882-1948." November 13, 2014. http://www.jewishagency.org/historical-aliyah/content/28841 (accessed July 2, 2018).

Jewish News Syndicate. "Study Finds Major Israeli Supreme Court Procedural Discrimination in Favor of Pro-Palestinian Plaintiffs." June 28, 2018. https://www.jns.org/study-finds-major-israeli-supreme-court-procedural-discrimination-in-favor-of-pro-palestinian-plaintiffs/ (accessed July 3, 2018).

Jewish Telegraph Agency. "U.S. Will Deduct $437 Million in Loans Because of Settlements." October 5, 1993. http://archive.jta.org/1993/10/05/archive/u-s-will-deduct-437-million-in-loans-because-of-settlements (accessed May 25, 2018).

Jewish Virtual Library. "Israel-Arab Peace Process: The Khartoum Resolutions (September 1, 1967)," https://www.jewishvirtuallibrary.org/the-khartoum-resolutions (accessed May 27, 2018).

———. "Lyndon Johnson Administration: Administration Alarmed by Israeli Settlement Plans." April 8, 1968. http://www.jewishvirtuallibrary.org/administration-alarmed-by-israeli-settlement-plans-april-1968 (accessed May 25, 2018).

———. "Ronald Reagan (1911-2004)." 2008. https://www.jewishvirtuallibrary.org/ronald-reagan (accessed May 25, 2018).

Kedar, Alexandre (Sandy). "The Legal Transformation of Ethnic Geography: Israeli Law and the Palestinian Landholder, 1948–1967." *New York University Journal of International Law and Politics* 33, no. 4 (Summer 2001): 923–1000.

Kerem Navot. "Israeli Settler Agriculture as a Means of Land Takeover in the West Bank." August 2013. http://rhr.org.il/heb/wp-content/uploads/Kerem-Navot.pdf (May 26, 2018).

Kessler, Glenn. "Israelis Claim Secret Agreement With U.S.: Americans Insist No Deal Made on Settlement Growth." *Washington Post*, April 24, 2008.

http://www.washingtonpost.com/wp-dyn/content/article/2008/04/23/AR2008042303128_pf.html (accessed May 26, 2018).

Kimmerling, Baruch. *Zionism and Territory: The Socio-Territorial Dimensions of Zionist Politics*. Berkeley: Institute of International Studies, University of California, 1983.

Kirkpatrick, Jeane J. "U.N. 'Mugging' Fails." *New York Times*, March 31, 1983, A23. http://www.nytimes.com/1983/03/31/opinion/un-mugging-fails.html (accessed May 26, 2018).

Kontorovich, Eugene. "Unsettled: A Global Study of Settlements in Occupied Territories." September 9, 2016. Revised January 17, 2018. *Journal of Legal Analysis* (2017): Northwestern Public Law Research Paper No. 16–20. https://ssrn.com/abstract=2835908; http://dx.doi.org/10.2139/ssrn.2835908 (accessed May 26, 2018).

Kontorovich, Eugene, and Penny Grunseid. "At the U.N., Only Israel Is an 'Occupying Power.'" *Wall Street Journal*, September 13, 2016. https://www.wsj.com/articles/at-the-u-n-only-israel-is-an-occupying-power-1473808544 (accessed May 26, 2018).

Kretzmer, David. *The Occupation of Justice: The Supreme Court of Israel and the Occupied Territories*. Albany: State University of New York Press, 2002.

Magid, Jacob. "Bill Stripping High Court's Power to Adjudicate West Bank Land Disputes Advances." *Times of Israel*, February 25, 2018. https://www.timesofisrael.com/bill-seizing-high-courts-power-to-adjudicate-west-bank-land-disputes-advances/ (accessed May 31, 2018).

———. "A Former Settler is Bent on Dismantling Outposts He Once Toiled to Establish." *Times of Israel*, January 12, 2018. https://www.timesofisrael.com/why-shabtay-bendet-is-working-to-dismantle-settlements-he-toiled-to-establish/ (accessed May 26, 2018).

Magid, Shaul. "West Bank Rabbi Menachem Froman's Zionist Post-Zionism, and What It Can Teach American Jews." August 4, 2016, *Tablet Magazine*. http://www.tabletmag.com/jewish-news-and-politics/192626/froman-zionist-post-zionism (accessed May 26, 2018).

Meron, Ya'akov. "Waste Land (Mewat) in Judea and Samaria." *ICLR: International and Comparative Law Review* 4, no. 1 (Spring 1981): 1–37. http://lawdigitalcommons.bc.edu/iclr/vol4/iss1/2 (accessed May 26, 2018).

Mitchell, George J. *The Negotiator: A Memoir*. New York: Simon & Schuster, 2015.

Norwegian Refugee Council, and Jehad Arafat, Mona Abed Al Aziz, Fatma Al Sharif, and Yaser Al Manama. "A Guide to Housing, Land and Property Law in the Gaza Strip." Edited by Elisabeth Koek, Martin Clutterbuck, and Alon Margalit. October 2015. https://www.nrc.no/globalassets/pdf/reports/a-guide-to-housing-land-and-property-law-in-the-gaza-strip-october-2015.pdf (accessed May 26, 2018).

Obama, Barack. "Text: Obama's Speech in Cairo." *New York Times*, June 4, 2009. http://www.nytimes.com/2009/06/04/us/politics/04obama.text.html?mcubz=3 (accessed May 26, 2018).

Obama White House Archives. "Remarks by President Obama and Prime Minister Netanyahu of Israel After Bilateral Meeting." Office of the Press Secretary, May 20, 2011. https://obamawhitehouse.archives.gov/the-press-office/2011/05/20/remarks-president-obama-and-prime-minister-netanyahu-israel-after-bilate (accessed June 3, 2018).

———. "Remarks by the President on the Middle East and North Africa." Office of the Press Secretary, May 19, 2011. https://obamawhitehouse.archives.gov/the-press-office/2011/05/19/remarks-president-middle-east-and-north-africa (accessed May 26, 2018).

Ongley, Frank, trans. *The Ottoman Land Code.* London: Forgotten Books, 2015.

Owen, Roger, ed. *New Perspectives on Property and Land in the Middle East.* Cambridge, MA: Center for Middle Eastern Studies, Harvard University Press, 2000.

Peace Now. "Methods of Confiscation—How Does Israel Justify and Legalize Confiscation of Lands? *Peace Now*, January 1, 2009. http://peacenow.org.il/en/methods-of-confiscation-how-does-israel-justify-and-legalize-confiscation-of-lands?lang=en (accessed May 26, 2018).

Phillips, David M. "The Illegal Settlements Myth." *Commentary*, December 1, 2009. https://www.commentarymagazine.com/articles/the-illegal-settlements-myth/ (accessed May 26, 2018).

Pileggi, Tamar. "Shaked Revives Bid to Extend Civil Law to Settlements." *Times of Israel*, May 2, 2016. http://www.timesofisrael.com/shaked-to-revive-bill-to-extend-civil-law-to-settlements/ (accessed May 26, 2018).

Rabi, Isidor Isaac. Quoted in Letter to the Editor, by Donald Sheff, "Issy, Did You Ask a Good Question Today?" *New York Times*, January 19, 1988, A26, https://mobile.nytimes.com/1988/01/19/opinion/l-izzy-did-you-ask-a-good-question-today-712388.html (accessed June 4, 2018).

Reagan, Ronald. "Reagan Outlines His Stands on Jewish Settlements." *New York Times*, September 9, 1982, A10. http://www.nytimes.com/1982/09/09/world/reagan-outlines-his-stand-on-jewish-settlements.html (accessed May 26, 2018).

———. Presidential Library. "Address to the Nation on United States Policy for Peace in the Middle East." KNBC-TV, Burbank, CA, September 1, 1982. https://www.reaganlibrary.archives.gov/archives/speeches/1982/90182d.htm (accessed May 26, 2018).

Regional and Local Councils of Judea & Samaria. June 22, 2017. Legal Advisor of Judea and Samaria. http://www.law.idf.il/163-6731-en/Patzar.aspx?SearchText=state land (accessed May 26, 2018).

Rosen, Steven J. "Israeli Settlements, American Pressure, and Peace." *Jewish Political Studies Review* 24, nos. 1–2 (Spring 2012): 32-44. http://jcpa.org/wp-content/uploads/2012/07/Rosen.pdf (accessed May 26, 2018).

———. "Obama's Foolish Settlements Ultimatum." *Middle East Forum*, April 1, 2010. http://www.meforum.org/2630/obama-settlements-ultimatum (accessed May 26, 2018).

Rosenberg, Yair. "The Most Anti-Israel President." *Tablet Magazine*, April 10, 2012. http://www.tabletmag.com/jewish-news-and-politics/96492/the-most-anti-israel-president (accessed May 27, 2018).

Rostow, Nicholas. "Are the Settlements Illegal?" *American Interest* 5, no. 4 (March 1, 2010). https://www.the-american-interest.com/2010/03/01/are-the-settlements-illegal/ (accessed May 27, 2018).

S. Daniel Abraham Center for Middle East Peace. "Is Peace Possible?" Launch event with former United States Special Envoy to the Middle East, Senator George J. Mitchell, January 12, 2011. http://www.centerpeace.org/events/peace-possible-launch-event-former-united-states-special-envoy-middle-east-senator-george-j-mitchell/ (accessed May 27, 2018).

Schnur-Levine, Ronit. "Private Property and Public: Power In the Occupied West Bank." *European Property Law Journal* 6, no. 2 (August 2017): 122–41.

Schechter, Asher. "Rebbe With a Cause: The Unconventional Truths of Menachem Froman." *Haaretz*, March 6, 2013. http://www.haaretz.com/israel-news/rebbe-with-a-cause-the-unconventional-truths-of-menachem-froman.premium-1.507710 (accessed May 27, 2018).

Schwebel Stephen M. "What Weight to Conquest." *American Journal of International Law* 64, no. 2 (April 1970): 344–47.

Scranton, William W. "Excerpts From Scranton's U.N. Speech." *New York Times*, March 25, 1976. http://www.nytimes.com/1976/03/25/archives/excerpts-from-scrantons-un-speech.html (accessed May 26, 2018).

Shani, Ayelett. "West Bank's Rabbi Menachem Froman Has the Solution to the Conflict." *Haaretz*, July 20, 2012. http://www.haaretz.com/israel-news/the-west-bank-s-rabbi-menachem-froman-has-the-solution-to-the-conflict-1.452325 (accessed May 27, 2018).

Sharvit Baruch, Pnina. "Security Council Resolution 2234: Legal Significance." *IISS*, Insight No. 883, December 30, 2016. http://www.inss.org.il/publication/security-council-resolution-2334-legal-significance/ (accessed May 27, 2018).

Smith, Barbara J. *The Roots of Separatism in Palestine: British Economic Policy, 1920-1929*, Syracuse, NY: Syracuse University Press, 1993.

Stein, Kenneth W. *Heroic Diplomacy: Sadat, Kissinger, Carter, Begin and the Quest for Arab Israeli Peace*. New York: Routledge, 1999.

Stone, Julius. *Israel and Palestine: Assault on the Law of Nations*. Baltimore: Johns Hopkins University Press, 1981.

Tawil, Bassam. "The Real Illegal Settlements." *Gatestone Institute*, December 5, 2016. https://www.gatestoneinstitute.org/9490/illegal-settlements (accessed May 27, 2018).

TOI Staff. "Full text of Nikki Haley's 2 speeches at UN Security Council debate on Jerusalem." *Times of Israel*, December 18, 2017. Last updated December 19, 2017. https://www.timesofisrael.com/full-text-of-nikki-haleys-speech-at-un-security-council-debate-on-jerusalem/ (accessed May 27, 2018).

Tomeh, Khaled Abu. "Are Settlements the Major Obstacle to Peace?" *Gatestone Institute*, April 12, 2012. https://www.gatestoneinstitute.org/3008/settlements-obstacle-to-peace (accessed June 3, 2018).

United Nations. *Charter of the United Nations*. June 26, 1945. http://www.un.org/en/charter-united-nations/index.html (accessed May 25, 2018).

———. Information System on the Question of Palestine (UNISPAL). "Palestine: The Palestine Order in Council." August 10, 1922. https://unispal.un.org/DPA/DPR/unispal.nsf/0/C7AAE196F41AA055052565F50054E656 (accessed May 27, 2018).

———. Security Council. General Assembly 32nd sess.,Official Records. "Resolution 446 (1979) 22 of March 1979." S/RES/446 (1979). https://unispal.un.org/DPA/DPR/unispal.nsf/db942872b9eae454852560f6005a76fb/ba123cded3ea84a5852560e50077c2dc?OpenDocument (accessed May 27, 2018).

———. Security Council 6484th Meeting. "Security Council Fails to Adopt Text Demanding That Israel Halt Settlement Activity as Permanent Member Casts Negative Vote." SC/10178, February 18, 2011. https://www.un.org/press/en/2011/sc10178.doc.htm.

United States. Ambassador to Israel: Interview with Israeli Walla. "The Administration Will Present the Peace Plan Within a Few Months." Walla News Channel, September 28, 2017. https://news.walla.co.il/item/3100410 (accessed May 27, 2018).

United States. National Archives and Records Administration. "Airgram From the Department of State to the Embassy in Israel." RG 59, Foreign Relations of the United States, 1964-1968, vol. 20, Arab-Israeli Dispute, 1967–1968, Document 137. https://history.state.gov/historicaldocuments/frus1964-68v20/d137 (accessed June 3, 2018).

Yiftachel, Oren. "The Law That Exposes Israel's True Colonialist Colors." *Haaretz. Opinoin*, December 14, 2016. http://www.haaretz.com/opinion/.premium-1.758794?=&ts=_1500979116702 (accessed May 27, 2018).

Yost, Charles. "U.S. Ambassador's Statement in the Security Council." In *The Jerusalem Question and Its Resolution: Selected Documents*, ed. Ruth Lapîdôt and Moshe Hirsch, 237. Dordrecht, Boston and London: Martinus Nijhoff; Jerusalem Institute for Israel, 1994.

Wilner, Michael. "US Consistent Against Settlements—And Against UN as Appropriate Venue." *Jerusalem Post, Analysis*, December 25, 2016. http://www.jpost.com/Israel-News/Politics-And-Diplomacy/Analysis-US-consistent-against-settlements-and-against-UN-as-appropriate-venue-476504 (accessed May 27, 2018).

Yahel, Havatzelet. "Land Disputes Between the Negev Bedouin and Israel." *Israel Studies* 11, no. 2 (2006): 1–14. http://weblaw.haifa.ac.il/he/Faculty/Kedar/lecdb/landregime/112.pdf (accessed May 25, 2018).

Yonah, Jeremy Bob. "50 Years Since 1967: What is the West Bank's Real Legal Status." *Jerusalem Post*, May 26, 2017. https://www.jpost.com/Magazine/50-years-of-law-versus-reality-493859 (accessed May 27, 2018).

Yonah, Jeremy Bob, and Lazarkoff Tovah. "Court: Israeli Government Must Defend Law Seizing Palestinian Property." *Jerusalem Post*, December 4,

2017. http://www.jpost.com/Israel-News/High-Court-issues-interim-order-on-Settlements-Law-516970 (accessed May 27, 2018).

Zunes, Stephen. "How Clinton and the Democrats Made Possible Israel's Settlements Expansion." *Huffington Post*, July 16, 2009. http://www.huffingtonpost.com/stephen-zunes/how-clinton-and-the-democ_b_212292.html (accessed May 27, 2018).

Index

About the Author

Martin Blecher is a Political Scientist in Sweden. He lectures and writes frequently about the Swedish-Israeli relations. His articles have been published in *Jerusalem Post* and *Israel National News*, as well as in Swedish newspapers. His previous book, *Vem säger vad?: röster för och emot tvåstatslösning mellan Israel och Palestina* (Roos & Tegner, 2017), was an anthology which contained views of proponents versus opponents to the "Two State Solution" between Israel and Palestine.

Lightning Source UK Ltd.
Milton Keynes UK
UKHW04f0753051018
330011UK00001B/58/P

9 780761 870647